Live Like David

DAILY DEVOTIONAL JOURNAL

Live Like David: Daily Devotional Journal Volume One
Copyright © 2024 by Israel365
All rights reserved.

For sales inquiries, contact: store@israel365.com

By Rabbi Elie Mischel and Shira Schechter
Cover and interior design by the Virtual Paintbrush

ISBN 978-1-957109-63-3

First Edition 2024

www.Israel365.com

ISRAƐL365

Live Like David

DAILY DEVOTIONAL JOURNAL

Teachings from the Book of Psalms

VOLUME 1

RABBI ELIE MISCHEL AND SHIRA SCHECHTER

Table of Contents

Introduction

I n the annals of history, few figures stand as tall as King David—shepherd, warrior, king, and most notably, the sweet singer of Israel. Through the Book of Psalms, David bared his soul, expressing the full spectrum of human emotions and experiences while maintaining an unwavering connection to God. In David, we find a model of how to live a life of deep faith and conviction, always turning to God in both moments of joy and in times of distress. His words continue to inspire, guiding us on how to approach our daily lives with the same trust, humility, and strength that David himself embodied.

The *Live Like David: Daily Devotional Journal* has been crafted as a continuation of the spiritual journey begun with our previous work, *Pray Like David*. In *Pray Like David*, we provided you with the tools to recite the Psalms in their authentic Hebrew form, preserving the beauty and sanctity of David's original words, while making them accessible to all through English transliteration and translation.

Now, with this daily devotional journal, we invite you to take this journey one step further. Each day, you will be guided through a single verse from the Psalms—verses that have been carefully chosen for their depth and relevance to daily life.

But this journal is more than just a continuation; it is a deepening of your connection to the wisdom of King David. Each verse is paired with a teaching that offers insights into David's thoughts and intentions, bringing his profound wisdom into our contemporary world. Alongside these teachings, you will find a journal prompt—a space for personal reflection, to record your thoughts, prayers, and how the verse speaks to you in your unique circumstances.

While we encourage you to use this journal as a daily guide—one verse, one teaching, and one reflection at a time—this journey is yours. There is no right or wrong way to engage with these sacred texts. Some days you may find yourself lingering on a single verse, while on others, you may be inspired to move through several. The goal is not speed but depth, allowing the words of David to permeate your life, helping you to cultivate a heart that, like his, is forever turned towards God.

As Jews who are blessed to live in the hills of Judea where David once walked, we feel a deep connection to these sacred teachings and are honored to share them with you. Our hope is that through this journal, we will join together in learning to think like David, pray like David, and ultimately, to live like David.

May this journey bring you strength, inspiration, and a deeper connection to the Eternal One.

Blessings,
Shira Schechter & Rabbi Elie Mischel

True Happiness

*"Happy is the man who has not followed the
counsel of the wicked, or taken the path of
sinners, or joined the company of the insolent."*

PSALMS 1:1

*ash-ray ha-EESH a-SHER LO ha-LAKH ba-a-TZAT
r'-sha-EEM uv-DE-rekh KHA-ta-eem LO a-MAD
uv-mo-SHAV lay-TZEEM LO ya-SHAV*

Meir Leibush (or the Malbim) understands the concept of "happiness" in spiritual terms, distinct from worldly "success." According to the psalmist, true happiness comes from cultivating refined character and spiritual qualities, avoiding intentional sins and desires and not indulging in laziness, which leads to moral stagnation.

R eflect on the difference between spiritual happiness and worldly success in your own life. In what ways do you seek happiness beyond material achievements? Do qualities like character development, self-discipline, and avoiding harmful desires play a role in your sense of fulfillment? Consider moments when you've felt morally "stagnant"—what contributed to that feeling, and how did (or could) you overcome it?

Comfort in Correction

"Though I walk through a valley of deepest darkness, I fear no harm, for You are with me; Your rod and Your staff—they comfort me."

PSALMS 23:4

GAM kee ay-LAYKH b'-GAY tal-MA-vet lo ee-RA RA kee a-TAH i-ma-DEE shiv-t'-KHA u-mish-an-TE-kha HAY-mah y'-na-kha-MU-nee

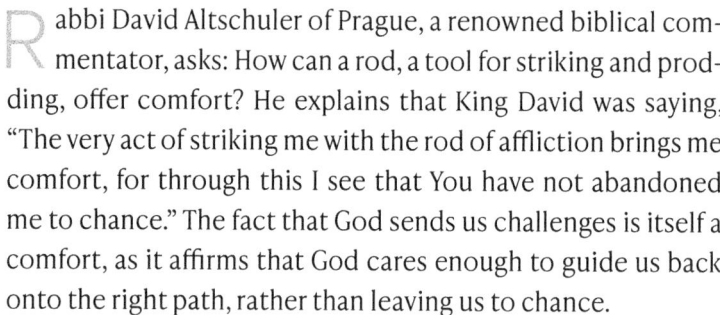

Rabbi David Altschuler of Prague, a renowned biblical commentator, asks: How can a rod, a tool for striking and prodding, offer comfort? He explains that King David was saying, "The very act of striking me with the rod of affliction brings me comfort, for through this I see that You have not abandoned me to chance." The fact that God sends us challenges is itself a comfort, as it affirms that God cares enough to guide us back onto the right path, rather than leaving us to chance.

C onsider a time in your life when you faced a challenge or hardship. In hindsight, did that difficulty guide you toward personal growth or a better path? How does the idea that challenges might be a form of guidance or care resonate with you?

Silent Prayer

"A maskil of David, while he was in the cave.
A prayer."

PSALMS 142:1

mas-KEEL l'-da-VID bih-yo-TO va-m'-a-RAH t'-fi-LAH

Rabbi Shimshon David Pincus noted that when David composed Psalm 142, he was concealed in a cave, evading King Saul and his men. In such a predicament, it was impossible for David to call out to God vocally, lest he reveal his position. Thus, his plea for mercy was a quiet, internal one. Yet, despite the silence of his words, the depth of his heart's cry resonated with God.

Consider the idea of internal versus external expressions when seeking help or mercy. How do you typically express your needs to others and to God? How do you cultivate a deeper connection with yourself or the Divine in moments of quiet reflection?

Gratitude in Grief

"A psalm for praise. Raise a shout for the Lord, all the earth."

PSALMS 100:1

miz-MOR l'-to-DAH ha-REE-u la-do-NAI kol ha-A-retz

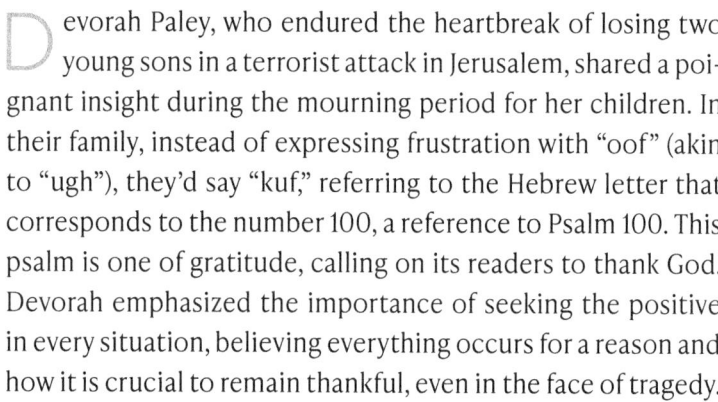

Devorah Paley, who endured the heartbreak of losing two young sons in a terrorist attack in Jerusalem, shared a poignant insight during the mourning period for her children. In their family, instead of expressing frustration with "oof" (akin to "ugh"), they'd say "kuf," referring to the Hebrew letter that corresponds to the number 100, a reference to Psalm 100. This psalm is one of gratitude, calling on its readers to thank God. Devorah emphasized the importance of seeking the positive in every situation, believing everything occurs for a reason and how it is crucial to remain thankful, even in the face of tragedy.

Devorah Paley's sons chose to use the word "kuf" as a reminder to be thankful even in their "oof" moments. What symbols or practices could you incorporate into your daily life to remind yourself to find gratitude even on difficult days?

Living in Today

"Today, if you listen to His voice."
PSALMS 95:7

ha-YOM im b'-ko-LO tish-MA-u

Serving God might seem overwhelming at first—where to start, how to achieve all that we aspire to within our limited time on Earth. The Psalmist offers a grounding perspective: "Today, if you listen to His voice" (Psalms 95:7). This teaches us the importance of living in the present, focusing on serving God today rather than getting caught up in what tomorrow or next year might bring. This verse also encourages us not to delay our spiritual duties to a future that is uncertain.

W hat are some actions you can take today to enhance your spiritual or personal growth, rather than putting them off for the future?

Waiting with Certainty

"I am more eager for the Lord than watchmen for the morning, watchmen for the morning."

PSALMS 130:6

naf-SHEE la-do-NAI mi-sho-m'-REEM la-BO-ker sho-m'-REEM la-BO-ker

Those who await redemption are likened to watchmen waiting for the morning. The biblical commentator known as the Malbim explains that just as these watchmen are certain that the morning will come despite the wait, so too, we can be assured that God's salvation will arrive at the appointed time.

Reflect on a time when you had to wait for something important. How did you maintain hope or faith during the waiting period?

Joy with Reverence

"Serve the Lord with fear,
and rejoice with quaking."

PSALMS 2:11

iv-DU et a-do-NAI b'-yir-AH v'-GEE-lu bir-a-DAH

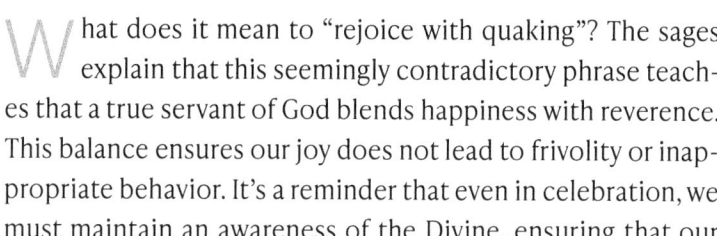

What does it mean to "rejoice with quaking"? The sages explain that this seemingly contradictory phrase teaches that a true servant of God blends happiness with reverence. This balance ensures our joy does not lead to frivolity or inappropriate behavior. It's a reminder that even in celebration, we must maintain an awareness of the Divine, ensuring that our joy is both deep and dignified.

R eflect on what it means to blend happiness with reverence in your own life. How do you maintain this balance during moments of joy or celebration?

Sleep in Peace

"I lay down and slept; I awoke, for the Lord will support me."

PSALMS 3:6

a-NEE sha-KHAV-tee va-ee-SHA-nah he-kee-TZO-tee
KEE a-do-NAI yis-m'-KHAY-nee

Sleep is essential yet it often alludes us. There are endless reasons why we don't get enough sleep, but sometimes it is our anxieties that keep us tossing and turning, searching for rest that seems just out of reach. Yet despite facing the life-threatening betrayal of his son Absalom, King David managed to lie down and sleep. His ability to rest amid such turmoil was rooted in his deep faith that God was his protector and support. David's experience illustrates how trust and faith can transcend anxiety and worry, allowing for tranquility even in the most challenging situations.

How do you cultivate a sense of security and peace, similar to King David, in your own life? Are there specific practices or thoughts that aid you?

Ask and Receive

"I the Lord am your God who brought you out
of the land of Egypt; open your mouth wide
and I will fill it."

PSALMS 81:11

*a-no-KHEE a-do-NAI e-lo-HE-kha ha-ma-al-
KHA may-E-retz mitz-RA-yim har-khev PEE-kha
va-a-mal-AY-hu*

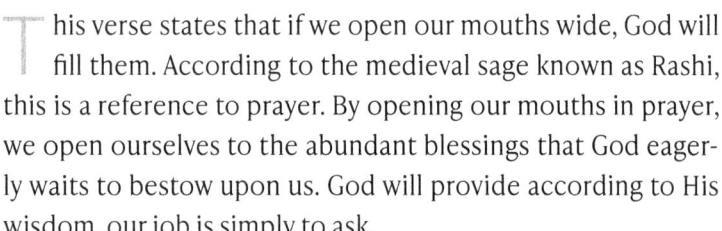

This verse states that if we open our mouths wide, God will fill them. According to the medieval sage known as Rashi, this is a reference to prayer. By opening our mouths in prayer, we open ourselves to the abundant blessings that God eagerly waits to bestow upon us. God will provide according to His wisdom, our job is simply to ask.

W rite about a time when you felt that your prayers were answered. How did this experience influence your faith or prayer habits?

A Cry from the Depths

"A song of ascents. Out of the depths I call You, O Lord."

PSALMS 130:1

SHEER ha-ma-a-LOT, mi-ma-a-ma-KEEM, k'-ra-TEE-kha, a-do-NAI.

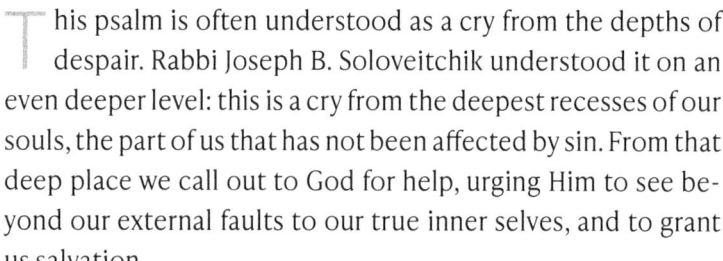

This psalm is often understood as a cry from the depths of despair. Rabbi Joseph B. Soloveitchik understood it on an even deeper level: this is a cry from the deepest recesses of our souls, the part of us that has not been affected by sin. From that deep place we call out to God for help, urging Him to see beyond our external faults to our true inner selves, and to grant us salvation.

R eflect on the idea that within each of us lies a pure, untouched part of the soul, unaffected by our mistakes or shortcomings. Consider how recognizing this inner purity might change the way you approach your own struggles or how you connect with others and the Divine. What are the core values or aspects of your identity that you turn to for strength and guidance?

Every Breath Counts

"Let every soul praise God. Hallelujah!"

PSALMS 150:6

KOL ha-n'-sha-MAH t'-ha-LAYL YAH ha-l'-lu-YAH

This verse is traditionally understood to mean that every soul should praise God. But the sages offer a homiletic twist by reading the word neshama, which means "soul," neshima, or "breath." This reading teaches that we should thank God for each breath that we take. Each breath is an opportunity to express gratitude and recognize God's presence in the most fundamental parts of our existence.

T oday, take a few moments to focus on your breathing. As you inhale and exhale, consider the automatic nature of this essential life process and reflect on the idea that each breath you take is a potential expression of gratitude and recognition of the Divine. How does this change your perception of this simple act? What are you grateful for today, and how can you use each breath as a reminder to appreciate these things?

Faith Through Night

"To proclaim Your steadfast love at daybreak,
Your faithfulness each night"

PSALMS 92:3

l'-ha-GEED ba-BO-ker khas-DE-kha ve-e-mu-na-t'-
KHA ba-lay-LOT

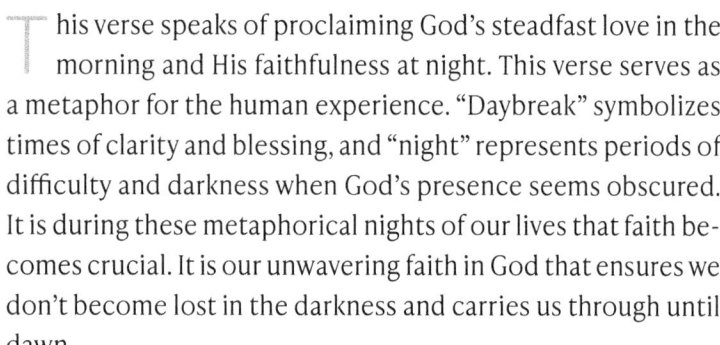

This verse speaks of proclaiming God's steadfast love in the morning and His faithfulness at night. This verse serves as a metaphor for the human experience. "Daybreak" symbolizes times of clarity and blessing, and "night" represents periods of difficulty and darkness when God's presence seems obscured. It is during these metaphorical nights of our lives that faith becomes crucial. It is our unwavering faith in God that ensures we don't become lost in the darkness and carries us through until dawn.

W hat personal trials have tested your faith, and how have you navigated them? In what ways can you nurture your faith to not only endure but thrive in adversity?

Freedom to Praise

"A psalm. A song; for the sabbath day."

PSALMS 92:1

miz-MOR SHEER l'-YOM ha-sha-BAT

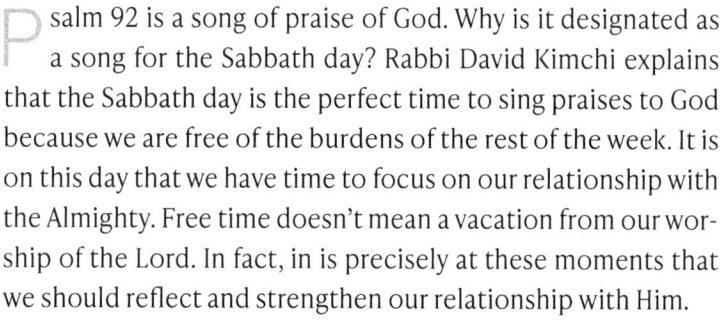

Psalm 92 is a song of praise of God. Why is it designated as a song for the Sabbath day? Rabbi David Kimchi explains that the Sabbath day is the perfect time to sing praises to God because we are free of the burdens of the rest of the week. It is on this day that we have time to focus on our relationship with the Almighty. Free time doesn't mean a vacation from our worship of the Lord. In fact, in is precisely at these moments that we should reflect and strengthen our relationship with Him.

W hat do you do during your free time? What is one way you can use that time to strengthen your relationship with the Almighty?

Sacred Rituals

"A psalm of David. A song for the dedication
of the House."

PSALMS 30:1

miz-MOR sheer kha-nu-KAT ha-BA-yit l'-da-VID

P salm 30 was originally written to be sung at the inaugu-
ration of the Temple. Today, we recite this psalm daily to
inaugurate our morning prayers which, the sages tell us, take
the place of the offerings that were brought in the Temple. This
reminds us of the enduring bond between our daily rituals and
the sacred traditions of our heritage.

Write about a specific moment in your life or in your prayers when you felt particularly connected to your ancestors and the continuity of your faith. How did this add meaning or enhance the experience?

Seeds of Joy

"They who sow in tears shall reap
with songs of joy."

PSALMS 126.5

ha-zo-r'-EEM b'-dim-AH b'-ri-NAH yik-TZO-ru

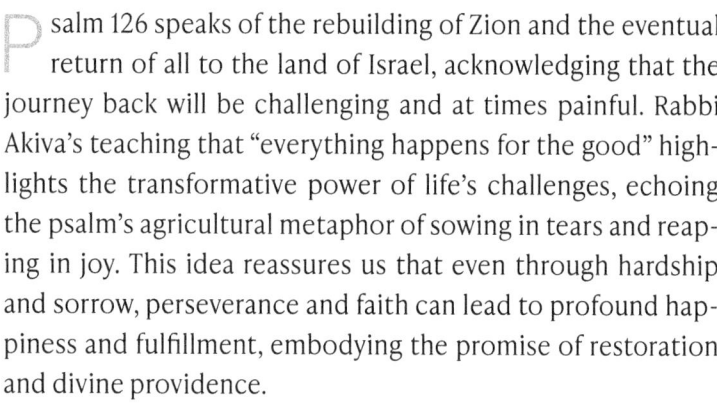

Psalm 126 speaks of the rebuilding of Zion and the eventual return of all to the land of Israel, acknowledging that the journey back will be challenging and at times painful. Rabbi Akiva's teaching that "everything happens for the good" highlights the transformative power of life's challenges, echoing the psalm's agricultural metaphor of sowing in tears and reaping in joy. This idea reassures us that even through hardship and sorrow, perseverance and faith can lead to profound happiness and fulfillment, embodying the promise of restoration and divine providence.

W rite about a time when you felt like you were "sowing in tears." How did this period of sowing help shape your future?

Clean Hands, Pure Heart

"He who has clean hands and a pure heart,
who has not taken a false oath by My life or
sworn deceitfully."

PSALMS 24:4

n'-KEE kha-PA-yim u-VAR lay-VAV a-SHER lo na-SA
la-SHAV naf-SHEE v'-lo nish-BA l'-mir-MAH

This is the answer the psalmist gives to the question "Who may ascend the mountain of the LORD? Who may stand in His holy place?" (Psalms 24:3). Bible scholar Amos Hakham explains that to come close to God, we must work on purifying our thoughts, our actions and our speech. Only one who works to perfect all of these areas will "carry away a blessing from the LORD, a just reward from God" (verse 5).

Write about specific steps you can take to work on perfecting your thoughts, actions, and speech. How do you think striving for this purity can bring you closer to God?

Love for the Helper

"The Lord restores sight to the blind; the Lord
makes those who are bent stand straight; the
Lord loves the righteous."

PSALMS 146:8

*a-do-NAI po-KAY-akh iv-REEM a-do-NAI zo-KAYF
k'-fu-FEEM a-do-NAI o-HAYV tza-dee-KEEM*

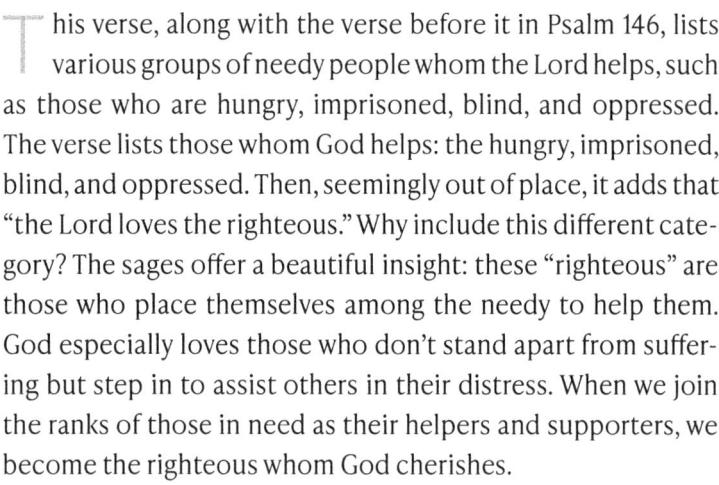

This verse, along with the verse before it in Psalm 146, lists various groups of needy people whom the Lord helps, such as those who are hungry, imprisoned, blind, and oppressed. The verse lists those whom God helps: the hungry, imprisoned, blind, and oppressed. Then, seemingly out of place, it adds that "the Lord loves the righteous." Why include this different category? The sages offer a beautiful insight: these "righteous" are those who place themselves among the needy to help them. God especially loves those who don't stand apart from suffering but step in to assist others in their distress. When we join the ranks of those in need as their helpers and supporters, we become the righteous whom God cherishes.

n what ways can you place yourself among the needy to support and uplift them? What is one way that you can support others in your daily life?

Brothers in Unity

"A song of ascents. Of David. How good and how pleasant it is that brothers dwell together."

PSALMS 133:1

SHEER ha-ma-a-LOT l'-da-VID hi-NAY mah TOV u-mah na-EEM SHE-vet a-KHEEM gam YA-khad

This verse emphasizes how beautiful and pleasant it is when brothers dwell together in harmony. According to the sages, the destruction of the Temple and the exile of the Jewish people were brought about by baseless hatred, as individuals began to focus on negativity and community leaders turned a blind eye to the injustices around them. The verse serves as a reminder of the power of unity and the dangers of discord within a community.

C onsider the concept of baseless hatred in a modern context. What steps can you take to cultivate empathy and respect in the interactions within your community?

The Miracle of Our Bodies

"I praise You, for I am awesomely,
wondrously made; Your work is wonderful;
I know it very well."

PSALMS 139:14

o-d'-KHA AL KEE no-ra-OT nif-LAY-tee nif-la-EEM
ma-a-SE-kha v'-naf-SHEE yo-DA-at m'-OD

David acknowledges that humans are created through wondrous miracles. Everything about us, from our formation in the womb and the birthing process to the functioning of our bodies, is miraculous. These words also imply that each and every one of us is a unique and wondrous being.

Reflect on what makes you unique and wonderful. How can you embrace and celebrate these qualities more fully? How does recognizing your own worth impact the way you live and interact with others?

The Miracles We Rarely Notice

"For the Lord is good; His steadfast love is eternal; His faithfulness is for all generations."

PSALMS 100:5

kee TOV a-do-NAI l'-o-LAM khas-DO v'-ad DOR va-DOR e-mu-na-TO

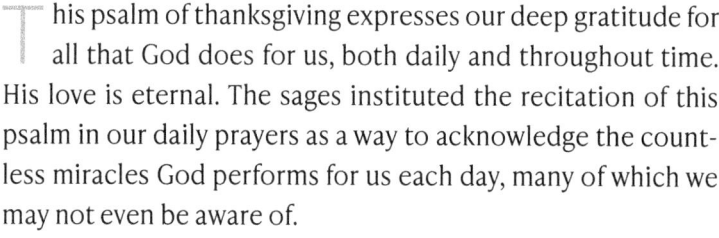

This psalm of thanksgiving expresses our deep gratitude for all that God does for us, both daily and throughout time. His love is eternal. The sages instituted the recitation of this psalm in our daily prayers as a way to acknowledge the countless miracles God performs for us each day, many of which we may not even be aware of.

Consider the countless miracles and blessings in your life. Write about a specific moment when you felt deeply grateful for God's presence and love in your life. How can you cultivate a greater sense of gratitude in your daily routine?

Desires of the Heart

"Seek the favor of the Lord, and He will grant you the desires of your heart."

PSALMS 37:4

v'-hit-a-NAG al a-do-NAI v'-yi-TEN l'-KHA mish-a-LOT li-BE-kha

K ing David advises us to trust in God and focus on doing good, rather than envying the wealth of the wicked, as true fulfillment comes from seeking God's favor. This verse highlights the importance of cultivating a relationship with God through devotion and service. When we seek His favor and place our faith in Him, He will grant the desires of our hearts, and our righteousness will become evident to all.

Reflect on what it means to seek the favor of the Lord in your life. How do your actions and intentions align with this pursuit? Consider how focusing on this relationship might influence the fulfillment of your deepest desires.

Under His Wings

"He will cover you with His pinions; you will find refuge under His wings; His fidelity is an encircling shield."

PSALMS 91:4

b'-ev-ra-TO YA-sekh LAKH v'-ta-khat k'-na-FAV tekh-SEH tzi-NAH v'-so-khay-RAH a-mi-TO

David assures us that God provides protection and comfort, much like a bird shelters its young under its wings. By trusting in God's faithfulness, we find a reliable refuge and a strong defense in times of trouble.

T hink about what 'refuge' means to you. Where do you find your safe haven during tough times? Reflect on the significance of feeling protected and how you can offer protection and support to others.

Secure in Faith

"Of David. The Lord is my light and my help; whom should I fear? The Lord is the stronghold of my life, whom should I dread?"

PSALMS 27:1

l'-da-VID a-do-NAI o-REE v'-yish-EE mi-MEE i-RA, a-do-NAI ma-OZ kha-YAI mi-MEE ef-KHAD

Rabbi Jonathan Sacks, former Chief Rabbi of the United Hebrew Congregations of the Commonwealth, wrote about this psalm, "no other psalm breathes so beautifully the quiet confidence of faith... Psalm 27 perfectly expresses our faith that God is sheltering us from harm and that nothing can make us afraid."

Reflect on a time in your life when you experienced a "quiet confidence of faith," similar to the assurance described in Psalm 27. How did this feeling manifest in your actions or thoughts? Write about how believing that you were protected or guided by a higher power influenced your approach to a challenging situation and whether it alleviated any fears you had.

Palm Tree Promise

"The righteous bloom like a date-palm; they thrive like a cedar in Lebanon."

PSALMS 92:13

tza-DEEK ka-ta-MAR yif-RAKH k'-E-rez ba-l'-va-NON yis-GEH

In this verse, King David compares a righteous person to a date palm tree, known in Hebrew as tamar. Just as the date palm produces numerous fruits, the deeds of a righteous person bear fruit. In addition, he enjoys a fruitful reward for his actions in both this world and the next.

Consider how this metaphor applies to your own life. Which of your actions or deeds do you feel are most fruitful? How do you see the rewards of these righteous actions manifesting in this world? Write about specific experiences where your good deeds have borne fruit and how you can continue to cultivate a life that is rich in righteousness.

Planted to Flourish

"Planted in the house of the Lord, they flourish
in the courts of our God."

PSALMS 92.14

*sh'-tu-LEEM b'-VAYT a-do-NAI b'-khatz-ROT e-lo-
HAY-nu yaf-REE-khu*

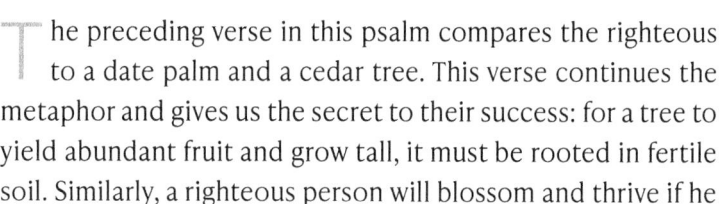

The preceding verse in this psalm compares the righteous to a date palm and a cedar tree. This verse continues the metaphor and gives us the secret to their success: for a tree to yield abundant fruit and grow tall, it must be rooted in fertile soil. Similarly, a righteous person will blossom and thrive if he is firmly planted in "God's House."

How do you interpret being "planted in God's House" in your own life? Write about the ways you currently cultivate your spiritual growth and how you might strengthen these practices.

Your Sacred Portion

"Delightful country has fallen to my lot; lovely indeed is my estate."

PSALMS 16:6

kha-va-LEEM na-f'-lu LEE ba-n'-i-MEEM af na-kha-LAT sha-f'-RAH a-LAI

I n the journey of life, we are each given a portion, a unique inheritance that is both a result of our efforts and a divine allotment. Just as the land of Israel was divided among the tribes with careful consideration and a divine lottery, so too are our lives a blend of our actions and the greater plan. We must strive to fulfill our potential while recognizing the hand of the Divine in our journey.

R eflect on the concept of inheritance in your life. What aspects of your life do you feel you have earned through your efforts, and where do you see the hand of a greater plan or divine guidance? How does this perspective influence your sense of purpose and direction?

At Home with God

"Only goodness and steadfast love shall pursue me all the days of my life, and I shall dwell in the house of the LORD for many long years."

PSALMS 23:6

AKH TOV va-KHE-sed yir-d'-FU-nee kol y'-MAY kha-YAI v'-shav-TEE b'-vayt a-do-NAI l-O-rekh ya-MEEM

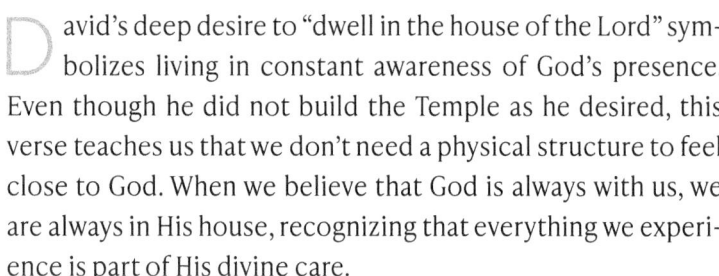

David's deep desire to "dwell in the house of the Lord" symbolizes living in constant awareness of God's presence. Even though he did not build the Temple as he desired, this verse teaches us that we don't need a physical structure to feel close to God. When we believe that God is always with us, we are always in His house, recognizing that everything we experience is part of His divine care.

R eflect on a time when you felt a strong sense of God's presence in your life. Has this influenced your perspective on everyday experiences and challenges? If so, write about how it has impacted you. What can you do to feel God's presence in your life more regularly?

The Perfect Shepherd

"A psalm of David. the Lord is my shepherd; I lack nothing."

PSALMS 23:1

miz-MOR l'-da-VID, a-do-NAI ro-EE lo ekh-SAR

David begins Psalm 23 by declaring that, because the Lord is his Shepherd, he lacks nothing. Just as a shepherd attentively tends to the needs of each sheep, God cares for every individual. Despite the many challenges David faced in his life, he remained content and trusting, confident that God knew exactly what he needed and provided for him at every moment.

How does the metaphor of the Lord as your shepherd resonate with you in as you navigate difficult times? Reflect on a specific instance where you felt His care guiding you.

Choose Your Companions Wisely

"Happy is the man who has not followed the counsel of the wicked, or taken the path of sinners, or joined the company of the insolent."

PSALMS 1:1

ash-RAY ha-EESH a-SHER LO ha-LAKH ba-a-TZAT r'-sha-EEM uv-DE-rekh KHA-ta-eem LO a-MAD uv-mo-SHAV lay-TZEEM LO ya-SHAV

This verse employs three verbs to describe how we should avoid the wicked: walk, stand, and sit. Rabbi David Kimchi advises that by steering clear of paths frequented by sinners, we can prevent the progression from merely walking alongside them to eventually joining and conforming to their ways. This guidance underscores the importance of carefully choosing our companions, especially for those seeking spiritual growth and a deeper connection with God.

R eflect on the relationships and environments you currently engage with in your daily life. Consider how these interactions influence your personal and spiritual growth. Have there been times when the company you kept or the places you frequented led you towards or away from the person you aspire to be? Write about these experiences and think about what changes, if any, you might want to make to align more closely with your values and goals.

Evergreen Virtues

"He is like a tree planted beside streams of water, which yields its fruit in season, whose foliage never fades, and whatever it produces thrives."

PSALMS 1:3

v'-ha-YAH k'-AYTZ sha-TUL al pal-gay MA-yim
a-SHER pir-YO yi-TAYN b'-i-TO v'-a-LAY-hu lo yi-BOL
v'-KHOL a-sher ya-a-SEH yatz-LEE-akh

I n this verse, a metaphor of a tree is used to describe the virtues of the righteous. Just as a healthy tree yields fruit at the expected time, so too does a righteous person deliver good deeds precisely when they are most needed. Similarly, like a tree whose leaves never wither, providing continual shade and relief to those around it, a righteous individual remains steadfast and ever-available to offer help and support to others. This enduring presence and reliability are hallmarks of their character, much like the evergreen leaves that shelter and protect.

ow do you provide support or relief to others? Are there moments when you feel you have delivered good deeds just when they were needed? Write about one of these instances and think about how you can consistently be a source of kindness and support to those who need it.

When Mountains Crumble

"Therefore we are not afraid though the earth reels, though mountains topple into the sea."

PSALMS 46:3

al KAYN lo NEE-ra b'-ha-MEER A-retz uv-MOT ha-REEM b'-LAYV ya-MEEM

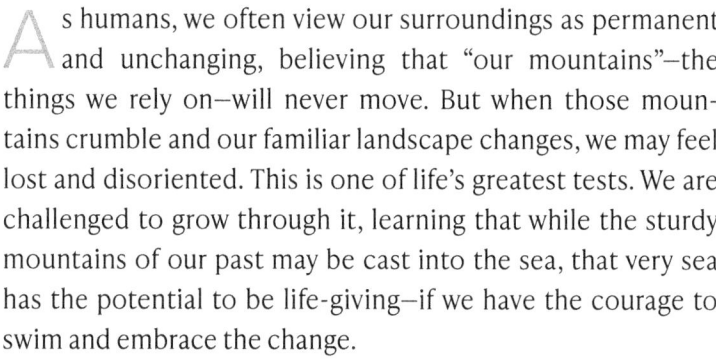

As humans, we often view our surroundings as permanent and unchanging, believing that "our mountains"—the things we rely on—will never move. But when those mountains crumble and our familiar landscape changes, we may feel lost and disoriented. This is one of life's greatest tests. We are challenged to grow through it, learning that while the sturdy mountains of our past may be cast into the sea, that very sea has the potential to be life-giving—if we have the courage to swim and embrace the change.

R eflect on a time in your life when something you thought was stable and unchanging suddenly shifted or was taken away. How did you react to this change? Did you feel disoriented or fearful, and how did you find your footing again?

He Never Stops Listening

"Evening, morning, and noon, I complain and moan, and He hears my voice."

PSALMS 55:18

E-rev va-VO-ker v'-tzo-ho-RA-yim a-see-KHA v'-e-he-MEH va-yish-MA ko-LEE

This verse highlights the continuous, unwavering nature of our communication with God. It reassures us that no matter how often we turn to Him with our worries and complaints, God is always listening. This demonstrates the depth of God's patience and love, encouraging us to maintain an open and honest dialogue with Him throughout all times of the day.

Reflect on the times in your life when you felt the need to turn to God in prayer or supplication. What are some ways you can incorporate regular moments of honest communication with God into your daily routine?

Safe in the Storm

*"Safe and sound, I lie down and sleep, for You
alone, O Lord, keep me secure."*

PSALMS 4:9

*b'-sha-LOM yakh-DAV esh-k'-VAH v'-ee-SHAN
kee a-TAH a-do-NAI l'-va-DAD la-VE-takh
to-shee-VAY-nee*

This verse beautifully conveys a sense of ultimate trust
and security in God. Despite the chaos of life, we can find
profound peace and rest in the assurance of God's protective
presence, just as a child feels safe under the watchful eye of a
loving parent.

Reflect on the sources of stress and anxiety in your life. How can a deeper trust in God's protection bring you peace? What practical steps can you take to cultivate this trust and find rest amidst turmoil?

There is Always a Way Home

"Many say of me, 'There is no deliverance for him through God. Selah."

PSALMS 3:3

ra-BEEM o-m'-REEM l'-naf-SHEE AYN y'-shu-A-tah LO vay-lo-HEEM SE-lah

This psalm was written by David as he fled from his son Absalom. David understood that Absalom's rebellion was a consequence of his sin with Bathsheba. In this verse, he reflects on how many people said to him, 'You took a married woman—there is no coming back from that!' But in the following verses, David expresses confidence in God's continued care, knowing that God never gives up on anyone. No matter what, there is always a way to return to Him.

ave you ever made a mistake that seemed unforgivable or irreversible? How did this affect your relationship with yourself, others, and God? Considering David's experience as he fled from Absalom and his confidence in God's continued care, write about how you can find hope and redemption even in your lowest moments.

When We Cannot See Clearly

"Had I not the assurance that I would enjoy the goodness of the Lord in the land of the living..."

PSALMS 27:13

lu-LAY he-e-MAN-tee lir-OT b'-TUV a-do-NAI b'-E-retz kha-YEEM

Rabbi Samson Raphael Hirsch explains this verse by suggesting that if not for the harm caused by the false witnesses mentioned in the previous verse, David would be able to perceive God's goodness in his present life, not just anticipate it in the afterlife. However, the distress caused by their accusations and slander clouds his ability to recognize God's blessings, prompting him to seek divine help against these adversaries.

Reflect on a time when you felt unfairly treated or misunderstood by others, and how it affected your outlook or belief in positive outcomes. Write about how you coped with these challenges and whether you sought support, perhaps even spiritual support, to help you through it. Consider what it might take for you to move past such obstacles and see the goodness in your life more clearly.

The Wonders of the Heavens

"The heavens declare the glory of Hashem, the sky proclaims His handiwork."

PSALMS 19:2

ha-sha-MA-yim m'-sa-p'-REEM k--VOD AYL u-ma-a-SAY ya-DAV ma-GEED ha-ra-KEE-a

Rabbi David Kimchi teaches that the wonders of the heavens, such as the sun, moon, and stars, reveal God's greatness and majesty. By observing the beauty and order of creation, we come to recognize and appreciate the power and wisdom of the Creator.

T hink about a moment when you were struck by the beauty of the natural world. How does this reinforce your faith in God's presence and creativity? What steps can you take to appreciate and honor God's creation in your daily life?

Strange Gods Within

*"There shall not be a strange god within you;
you shall not bow to a foreign god."*

PSALMS 81:10

*lo yih-YEH v'-KHA AYL ZAR v'-LO tish-ta-kha-VEH
l'-AYL nay-KHAR*

What does it mean to have "strange gods" within you? The Sages explain that this refers to uncontrolled anger. Anger can be devastating, leading us to act destructively and lose sight of God's providence and goodness. When anger overwhelms us, it becomes a destructive force, akin to serving foreign gods, clouding our judgment and corrupting our character. Like idolatry, uncontrolled anger signifies a departure from recognizing and honoring God's presence in our lives.

Reflect on a moment when you were overwhelmed by anger. How did this anger affect your actions and relationships? Consider steps you can take to manage and channel your anger in a healthier way, so it does not dominate your life or disrupt your spiritual path.

Our True Helper

"A song for ascents. I turn my eyes to the mountains; from where will my help come?"

PSALMS 121:1

SHEER la-ma-a-LOT e-SA ay-NAI el he-ha-REEM
may-A-yin ya-VO ez-REE

When we are in need of help, we often turn to the 'strong, tall mountains' in our lives, hoping they can assist us. These mountains may represent various sources of perceived strength and support, such as influential people, wealth, power, or material possessions. Yet, as the next verse reminds us, true help comes only from the Lord. Ultimately, it is not the 'tall mountains' or physical things in this world we can truly rely on; only God is our true source of help.

T hink about the "mountains" in your life—those people, possessions, or sources of strength that you often turn to in times of need. How do these compare to your reliance on God? Reflect on a time when you depended on something other than God for support, and how the outcome may have changed if you had turned to Him first. What does it mean for you to fully trust in God's help over worldly sources of strength?

Wake from Dreaming

"A song of ascents. When the Lord returns the returnees to Zion, we shall be like dreamers."

PSALMS 126:1

SHEER ha-ma-a-LOT b'-SHUV a-do-NAI et shee-VAT tzi-YON ha-YEE-nu k'-khol-MEEM

R abbi Chaim Drukman uses a metaphor to explain this verse. Imagine a student sitting in class, his eyes open but his mind drifting far away, disconnected from the lesson. Similarly, during the modern return to Zion, many people are "daydreaming," unable to fully grasp or appreciate the magnitude of the events unfolding before us. After 2,000 years of exile and suffering, the re-establishment of a Jewish state is a profound miracle, yet so many are caught up in their own concerns and do not internalize the significance of this historic moment. We must open our eyes and hearts to the extraordinary blessings of our time.

D o you recognize God's hand in historical events taking place in our generation. How can you stay attentive to the unfolding of remarkable changes in the world around you?

Already Answered

"But I trust in Your faithfulness, my heart will exult in Your deliverance. I will sing to the Lord, for He has been good to me."

PSALMS 13:6

va-a-NEE b'-khas-d'-KHA va-takh-TEE ya-GAYL li-BEE bee-shu-a-TE-kha a-SHEE-rah la-do-NAI KEE ga-MAL a-LAI

This verse presents a notable shift from future to past tense. Instead of saying, 'I will sing to the Lord, for He will be good to me,' the psalmist asserts, 'for He has been good to me,' using the past tense. This change reflects a transformation in the one praying, rather than in their circumstances. Although the psalmist does not know the outcome of his prayers or how they will be received by God, the act of praying itself brings happiness and joy, drawing him closer to the Almighty. This closeness is, in itself, a form of salvation and a manifestation of divine goodness. Thus, even without knowing how his prayers will be answered, he has already received a profound reward through the act of prayer. God has already been good to him.

How does the act of praying affect your state of mind and your relationship with God? Write about the emotions and thoughts you experience as you pray. Do your prayer bring you a sense of peace, joy, or closeness to the divine, regardless of the eventual outcome?

The Illusion of Power

> "On every side the wicked roam when baseness
> is exalted among men."
>
> PSALMS 12:9

*sa-VEEV r'-sha-EEM yit-ha-la-KHUN k'-RUM zu-LUT
liv-NAY a-DAM*

When baseness is exalted among men" refers to a situation where the wicked and their wickedness appear to be exalted. On the outside, they may seem great, powerful, and respected, but in reality, they are lowly, base, and empty, much like a blown-up balloon. The closer you get to them and the more you get to know them, the more you realize their true nature. Eventually, just like a balloon, their facade will burst.

DATE:

Reflect on a time when someone or something that appeared powerful and respected turned out to be empty and insubstantial. How did your perception change as you got closer and learned more about them? Write about the moment you realized their true nature and how it affected your understanding of appearances versus reality. How can this experience guide you in recognizing true value and integrity in people and situations in the future?

The People Who Sacrifice

"For the holy ones who are in the land, and the mighty ones in whom is all my delight."

PSALMS 16:3

lik-do-SHEEM a-SHER ba-A-rez HAY-mah v'-a-dee-RAY kol khef-tzee VAM

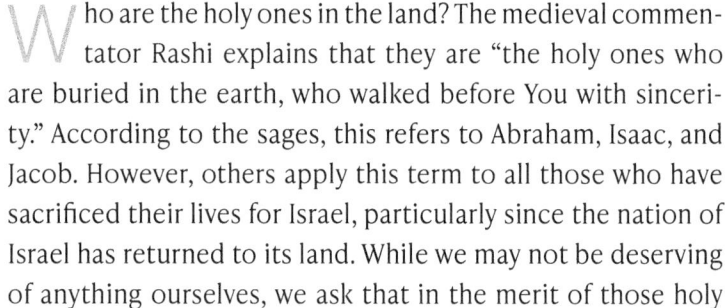

Who are the holy ones in the land? The medieval commentator Rashi explains that they are "the holy ones who are buried in the earth, who walked before You with sincerity." According to the sages, this refers to Abraham, Isaac, and Jacob. However, others apply this term to all those who have sacrificed their lives for Israel, particularly since the nation of Israel has returned to its land. While we may not be deserving of anything ourselves, we ask that in the merit of those holy people who gave their lives for the land of Israel, our prayers be answered.

Reflect on the sacrifices made by those who have given their lives for Israel throughout history. How do their acts of devotion and sacrifice influence your own sense of purpose and commitment?

Belief in a Divine Judge

"For the conductor, of David; The fool said in his heart, 'There is no God'; they have dealt corruptly; they have committed abominable deeds; no one does good."

PSALMS 14:1

lam-na-TZAY-akh l'-da-VID a-MAR na-VAL b'-li-BO AYN e-lo-HEEM hish-KHEE-tu hit-EE-vu a-lee-LAH AYN o-SAY TOV

Someone who behaves foolishly or boorishly towards others does so because they believe there is no God. Without belief in a divine Judge, they feel free to act without moral restraint or accountability. This lack of belief in divine judgment leads them to think they can act without facing any consequences.

Reflect on a time when you or someone you know acted corruptly towards others. What were the circumstances, and how did this behavior align with or contradict your belief in God's presence? Consider how a strong faith in God's guidance might influence how we treat others. How can deepening your relationship with God and fostering a sense of divine responsibility change your actions and interactions for the better?

Simple Steps to God

"A psalm of David. Lord, who may sojourn in Your tent, who may dwell on Your holy mountain?"

PSALMS 15:1

miz-MOR l'-da-VID a-do-NAI mee ya-GUR b'-o-ho-LE-kha mee yish-KON b'-HAR kod-SHE-kha

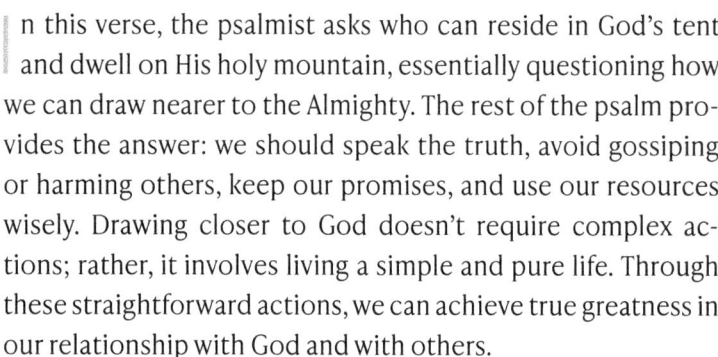

In this verse, the psalmist asks who can reside in God's tent and dwell on His holy mountain, essentially questioning how we can draw nearer to the Almighty. The rest of the psalm provides the answer: we should speak the truth, avoid gossiping or harming others, keep our promises, and use our resources wisely. Drawing closer to God doesn't require complex actions; rather, it involves living a simple and pure life. Through these straightforward actions, we can achieve true greatness in our relationship with God and with others.

Consider how living a pure and straightforward life might deepen your connection with the Almighty. What small changes can you make today to strengthen your relationship with God and achieve spiritual greatness?

Joy in God's Commands

"Your righteousness is perpetual
righteousness, and Your Torah is true."

PSALMS 119:142

*tzid-ka-t'-KHA TZE-dek l'-o-LAM v'-to-ra-t'-KHA
e-MET*

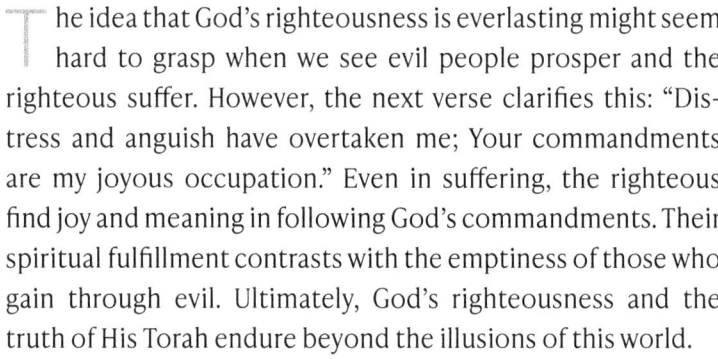

The idea that God's righteousness is everlasting might seem hard to grasp when we see evil people prosper and the righteous suffer. However, the next verse clarifies this: "Distress and anguish have overtaken me; Your commandments are my joyous occupation." Even in suffering, the righteous find joy and meaning in following God's commandments. Their spiritual fulfillment contrasts with the emptiness of those who gain through evil. Ultimately, God's righteousness and the truth of His Torah endure beyond the illusions of this world.

DATE:

R eflect on a time when you struggled to understand why injustice seemed to prevail, or when you saw sinners prosper while the righteous faced hardship. How does the idea that God's righteousness is everlasting help you find meaning in these moments?

A Time to Reflect

"You have visited me at night, probed my mind,
You have tested me and found nothing amiss;
I determined that my mouth
should not transgress."

PSALMS 17:3

ba-KHAN-ta li-BEE, pa-KAD-ta LAI-lah tz'-raf-TA-nee
val tim-TZA, za-mo-TEE bal ya-a-vor PEE.

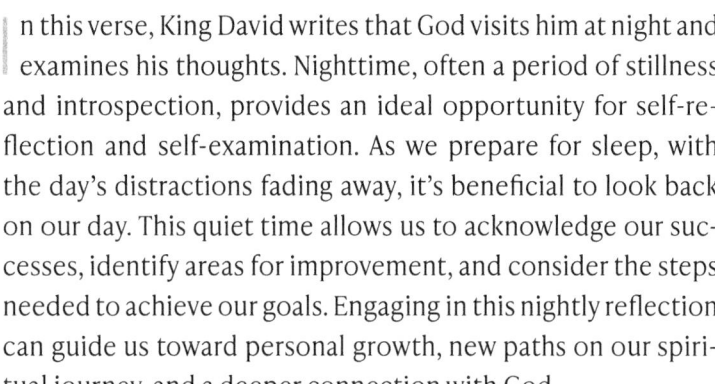

I n this verse, King David writes that God visits him at night and examines his thoughts. Nighttime, often a period of stillness and introspection, provides an ideal opportunity for self-reflection and self-examination. As we prepare for sleep, with the day's distractions fading away, it's beneficial to look back on our day. This quiet time allows us to acknowledge our successes, identify areas for improvement, and consider the steps needed to achieve our goals. Engaging in this nightly reflection can guide us toward personal growth, new paths on our spiritual journey, and a deeper connection with God.

Before you go to sleep tonight, take some time to reflect on your day. Consider the following questions: How did you feel God's presence in your life today? What were your successes, and what areas need improvement? What steps can you take to address these areas and move closer to your goals?

The Unshakeable Rock

*"Truly, who is a god except the LORD,
who is a rock but our God?"*

PSALMS 18:32

*KEE MEE e-lo-AH mi-bal-a-DAY a-do-NAI u-MEE
TZUR zu-la-TEE a-lo-HAY-nu*

Throughout life, things constantly change, and the unexpected can happen at any moment. David's life was particularly tumultuous: King Saul welcomed him into his palace only to turn on him, he spent much of his time in battle, and his own son tried to kill him. The only constant force in his life was God Himself. David recognized that God and His presence were the only things he could truly depend on, serving as his unwavering rock amidst the chaos.

Reflect on a time in your life when everything seemed uncertain and chaotic. How did you cope with the changes and unexpected events? Did your faith and reliance on God help you navigate through the turmoil? Write about how recognizing and relying on God's steadfast support can provide strength and stability in future challenging times.

_____

_____

_____

_____

_____

_____

_____

_____

_____

_____

_____

_____

_____

_____

_____

_____

_____

Gone in a Flash

"Man is like a breath; his days
are like a passing shadow."

PSALMS 144:4

a-DAM la-HE-vel da-MAH ya-MAV k'-TZAYL o-VAYR

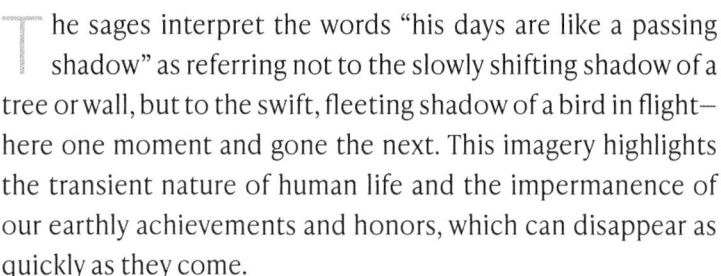

The sages interpret the words "his days are like a passing shadow" as referring not to the slowly shifting shadow of a tree or wall, but to the swift, fleeting shadow of a bird in flight—here one moment and gone the next. This imagery highlights the transient nature of human life and the impermanence of our earthly achievements and honors, which can disappear as quickly as they come.

Reflect on the transient nature of life. Consider how this perspective can influence your understanding of your daily actions, achievements, and relationships. How might embracing the impermanence of life change the way you live each day? Write about specific ways you can find meaning and fulfillment in the present moment, despite life's brevity.

Soar Again

"Who sates your mouth with goodness, that
your youth renews itself like the eagle."

PSALMS 103:5

*ha-mas-BEE-a ba-TOV ed-YAYKH tit-kha-DAYSH
ka-NE-sher n'-u-RAI-khee*

When a person recovers from illness, it's as if they regain the vigor of their youth. The eagle is a symbol of rejuvenation, shedding its old feathers and growing new ones. As Isaiah said, "But those who wait upon the Lord shall renew their strength, They shall rise up with wings as eagles..." (Isaiah 40:31).

Reflect on the symbolism of the eagle in Isaiah 40:31, and how it represents renewal and strength. Consider how this imagery can influence your perspective on overcoming challenges and recovering from difficult times. How might embracing the idea of rejuvenation, both physically and spiritually, shape the way you approach setbacks in your life? Write about specific ways you can cultivate resilience and find renewed strength in the face of adversity.

Family Not Foes

"For the conductor; of the servant of the Lord,
of David, who spoke to the Lord the words of
this song on the day that the Lord saved him
from the hand of all his enemies
and from the hand of Saul."

PSALMS 18:1

*lam-na-TZAY-akh l'-E-ved a-do-NAI l'-da-VID a-SHER
di-BER la-do-NAI et div-RAY ha-shee-RAH ha-ZOT
b'-YOM hi-TZEEL a-do-NAI o-TO mi-KAF kol o-y'-VAV
u-mi-YAD sha-UL*

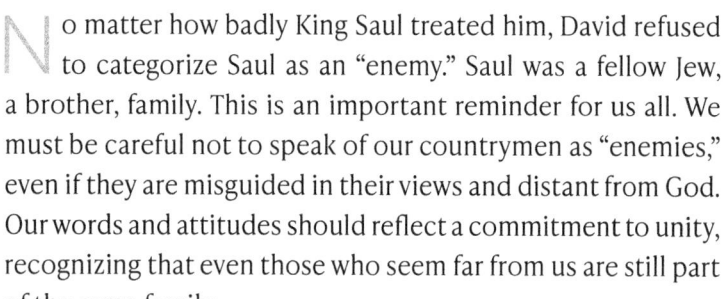

No matter how badly King Saul treated him, David refused to categorize Saul as an "enemy." Saul was a fellow Jew, a brother, family. This is an important reminder for us all. We must be careful not to speak of our countrymen as "enemies," even if they are misguided in their views and distant from God. Our words and attitudes should reflect a commitment to unity, recognizing that even those who seem far from us are still part of the same family.

Reflect on a time when you found it difficult to see someone as anything other than an adversary. How might your perspective change if you were to view this person as a brother, family, or part of a shared community, even in the face of disagreement? Write about how adopting this mindset could alter your interactions and relationships, especially with those whose views differ from your own.

Word Above Wonders

"The law of the Lord is perfect, restoring the
soul; the testimony of the Lord is faithful,
making the simple one wise."

PSALMS 19:8

*to-RAT a-do-NAI t'-mee-MAH m'-shee-VAT NA-fesh
ay-DUT a-do-NAI ne-e-ma-NAH makh-KEE-mat
PE-tee*

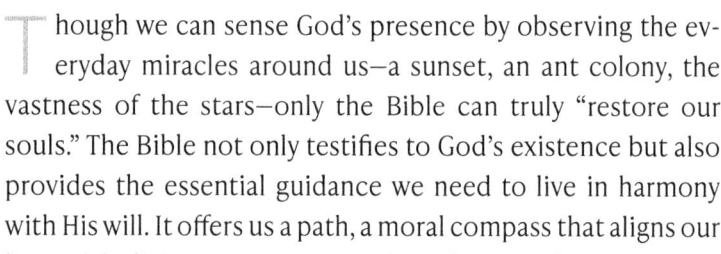

Though we can sense God's presence by observing the everyday miracles around us—a sunset, an ant colony, the vastness of the stars—only the Bible can truly "restore our souls." The Bible not only testifies to God's existence but also provides the essential guidance we need to live in harmony with His will. It offers us a path, a moral compass that aligns our lives with divine purpose, providing clarity and strength in a world that often feels chaotic and overwhelming.

DATE:

Consider how the teachings of the Bible have influenced your understanding of right and wrong, and how they guide your daily decisions. Write about a moment when a biblical principle helped you find clarity or peace in a challenging situation, and explore how you can deepen your reliance on these teachings to restore and strengthen your soul.

Unseen Providence

*"My God, my God, why have You forsaken me?
You are far from my salvation and from the
words of my moaning."*

PSALMS 22:2

ay-LEE ay-LEE la-MAH a-zav-TA-nee ra-KHOK mee-shu-a-TEE div-RAY sha-a-ga-TEE

With the fate of her people at stake, Esther approached King Ahasuerus to plead on their behalf. In doing so, she risked her life, for "any man or woman who comes to the king, into the inner court, who is not summoned, there is but one law for him, to be put to death, except the one to whom the king extends the golden scepter, that he may live" (Esther 4:11). As she took those fateful steps, the sages say she whispered Psalm 22 to God, feeling abandoned yet still placing her trust in Him. Though she feared God had forsaken her, in reality, His presence never wavered—He guided her every step, ensuring her success in saving her people.

Reflect on a time when you felt abandoned or alone in a difficult situation. How did you navigate that experience, and did you later realize that God or a higher power was guiding you through it? As you meditate on Psalm 22:2 and Esther's courage, consider how faith can sustain you even when you feel most forsaken. Write about ways you can cultivate trust in God's presence, especially during life's most challenging moments.

Keep Climbing

"If I ascend to the heavens, there You are,
and if I make my bed in the grave, behold,
You are there."

PSALMS 139:8

im e-SAK sha-MA-yim SHAM A-tah v'-a-tzee-AH sh'-OL hi-NE-ka

Repentance is a continual journey, not a destination. Whether you find yourself on an uplifting path or facing profound challenges, the key is to persistently seek God and remain dedicated to His ways. The journey of faith requires constant self-reinforcement and resilience. When you are at your peak, do not become complacent; always strive to deepen your connection with God. Conversely, if you fall into difficult times, do not succumb to despair.

Reflect on your journey of repentance and growth. Consider how you can encourage yourself during times of struggle and ensure that even in moments of ascent or descent, you continue to seek and strengthen your connection with God.

Join the Fight

"Who is this King of Glory? The Lord of Hosts-
He is the King of Glory forever."

PSALMS 24:10

MEE HU ZEH ME-lekh ha-ka-VOD a-do-NAI tz'-
va-OT HU ME-lekh ha-ka-VOD SE-lah

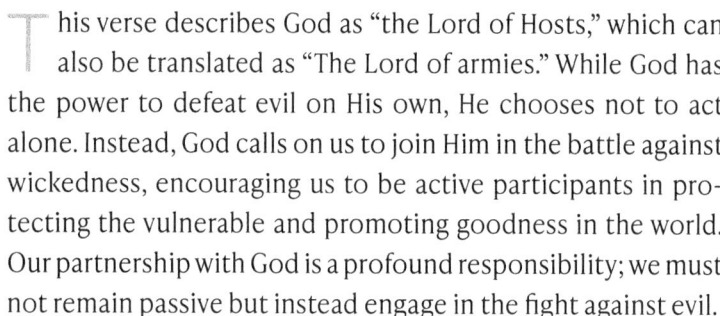

This verse describes God as "the Lord of Hosts," which can also be translated as "The Lord of armies." While God has the power to defeat evil on His own, He chooses not to act alone. Instead, God calls on us to join Him in the battle against wickedness, encouraging us to be active participants in protecting the vulnerable and promoting goodness in the world. Our partnership with God is a profound responsibility; we must not remain passive but instead engage in the fight against evil.

Reflect on how you can actively partner with God in the fight against evil and injustice. What are some specific ways you can contribute to protecting the vulnerable and promoting goodness in your daily life? Consider moments when you might have been passive in the face of wrongdoing. How can you become more engaged in standing up for righteousness and actively join in God's work to make the world a better place.

Suffering's Gift

"The troubles of my heart have increased;
deliver me from my straits."

PSALMS 25.17

tza-ROT l'-va-VEE hir-KHEE-vu mi-m'-tzu-ko-TAI
ho-tzee-AY-nee

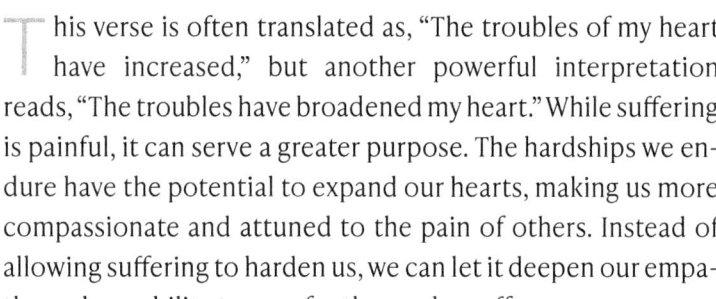

This verse is often translated as, "The troubles of my heart have increased," but another powerful interpretation reads, "The troubles have broadened my heart." While suffering is painful, it can serve a greater purpose. The hardships we endure have the potential to expand our hearts, making us more compassionate and attuned to the pain of others. Instead of allowing suffering to harden us, we can let it deepen our empathy and our ability to care for those who suffer.

R eflect on a time when you faced significant hardship. How did that experience change you? Consider how your own suffering has shaped your ability to empathize with others in pain. Write about ways in which your heart has broadened through the challenges you've faced, and how you can use this expanded empathy to support and uplift others.

The Heart's Deep Call

"On Your behalf, my heart says, 'Seek My presence' Your presence, O Lord, I will seek."

PSALMS 27:8

l'-KHA a-MAR li-BEE ba-k'-SHU fa-NAI et pa-NE-kha a-do-NAI a-va-KAYSH

This verse speaks to the deep, often unspoken yearning within our hearts for a connection with God. This inner longing is a call for us to reach out and seek Him, revealing that God is already present in the depths of our being. "God is the rock of my heart and my portion forever" (Psalm 73:27). Our hearts are not just yearning but are actively urging us to seek God's presence, affirming that He is ever-present within us, waiting for us to acknowledge and respond to His call.

onsider the inner yearnings of your heart and how they might reflect a deeper desire for connection with God. Reflect on moments when you felt a profound sense of longing or search for meaning. How does recognizing this inner call influence your spiritual practices and daily life? Write about how you can more intentionally seek God's presence and embrace the fulfillment that comes from recognizing Him as the rock and portion of your heart.

One World, One God

*"And the nations will fear the name of the Lord,
and all the kings of the earth Your glory."*

PSALMS 102:16

*v'-yee-r'-U go-YIM et SHAYM a-do-NAI v'-khol mal-
KHAY ha-A-retz et k'-vo-DE-kha*

This verse envisions a time when God's miracles will be so profound that they inspire all nations to recognize His divine power. We earnestly hope and pray for the time when all people on earth will return to God. We ask God to manifest wonders before the eyes of all nations, stirring them to fear His name and acknowledge His sovereignty. It is only through this universal recognition of God's divinity that His kingdom on earth will be fully realized.

Reflect on the steadfast faith in the God of Israel demonstrated by the people of Israel throughout history, even in the face of adversity. How does this unwavering devotion inspire your own spiritual journey? Consider how you can contribute to the broader vision of God's kingdom. Write about ways you can be a part of this greater mission, both through your personal faith and in encouraging others to recognize and honor God's power.

Count Your Blessings

"My soul, bless the Lord and do not forget any of His benefits."

PSALMS 103:2

ba-r'-KHEE naf-SHEE et a-do-NAI v'-AL tish-k'-KHEE kol g'-mu-LAV

G ratitude is the cornerstone of our service to God. The psalmist urges us not to overlook any of the countless benefits and acts of kindness that God has bestowed upon us. By remembering and acknowledging these blessings, we honor God and reinforce our relationship with Him. True devotion is reflected in our ability to express thanks for every favor, big or small, and to live a life that continually celebrates His goodness. This constant gratitude transforms our daily existence into an ongoing act of worship.

Take a moment to list specific blessings in your life, both major and minor. How can cultivating a mindset of gratitude enhance your spiritual practice and strengthen your relationship with God? Write about how recognizing and appreciating these blessings can shape your daily actions and interactions with others, fostering a deeper sense of connection and devotion.

Merit Through Pain

"May God answer you on a day of distress; may
the name of the God of Jacob fortify you."

PSALMS 20:2

*ya-an-KHA a-do-NAI b'-YOM tz-RAH y'-sa-GEV-kha
SHAYM e-lo-HAY ya-a-KOV*

Simply understood, this verse reassures us that even in
times of distress, when it feels as though God has turned
away, we should remember that He has not truly abandoned us.
However, the sages offer a deeper interpretation: our suffering
and trials actually create a merit that leads to God's response.
This perspective suggests that the very struggles we endure
are instrumental in drawing God's attention and support. Our
challenges are not without purpose; they are the catalyst for
divine intervention and help.

Reflect on a difficult time in your life when it felt like God was distant or absent. How might your perspective change if you viewed that struggle as a way of drawing God's attention and support? Consider how your challenges have been a catalyst for growth or deeper connection with God. How does this idea—that trials can create merit—affect how you view current or past hardships?

Holy Anger

"If only You would slay the wicked, O God, and
men of blood, 'Turn away from me.'"

PSALMS 139:19

*im tik-TOL e-LO-ah ra-SHA v'-an-SHAY da-MEEM
SU-ru ME-nee*

A t first glance, the psalmist's plea for the destruction of
the wicked may seem vengeful and unsettling. However,
a genuine concern for righteousness means we cannot be in-
different to the presence of evil. The psalmist's fervent desire
for justice highlights his deep commitment to moral integrity
and his strong reaction to wrongdoing. If the psalmist appears
more intense in his condemnation than others, it is a reflection
of his profound commitment to righteousness and his deep
sensitivity to moral corruption.

DATE:

Reflect on a time when you felt deeply disturbed by an injustice or wrongdoing. How did this reaction reveal your values and commitment to righteousness? Consider how your sensitivity to moral issues drives you to act and advocate for justice. Write about how you can use this awareness to confront and address wrongs in your own life and community, ensuring your response aligns with your principles and promotes positive change.

Excitement in Divine Service

"One thing I ask of the Lord, that I seek-that I may dwell in the house of the Lord all the days of my life, to see the pleasantness of the Lord and to visit His Temple every morning."

PSALMS 27:4

a-KHAT sha-AL-tee may-AYT a-do-NAI o-TAH a-va-KAYSH shiv-TEE b'-VAYT a-do-NAI kol y'-MAY kha-YAI la-kha-ZOT b'-no-am a-do-NAI ul-va-KAYR b'-hay-kha-LO

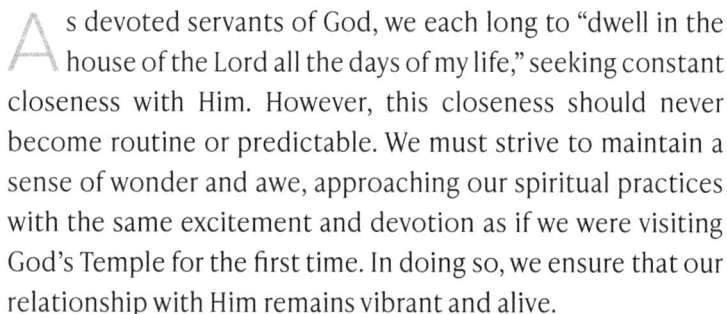

As devoted servants of God, we each long to "dwell in the house of the Lord all the days of my life," seeking constant closeness with Him. However, this closeness should never become routine or predictable. We must strive to maintain a sense of wonder and awe, approaching our spiritual practices with the same excitement and devotion as if we were visiting God's Temple for the first time. In doing so, we ensure that our relationship with Him remains vibrant and alive.

Reflect on your current relationship with God. Are there moments when your spiritual practice feels routine or lacking in enthusiasm? Write about how you can rekindle the excitement and reverence in your daily connection with God. Consider specific actions or changes that could help you experience your faith with renewed energy and passion, and explore ways to keep your spiritual journey engaging and meaningful each day.

When Parents Can't Help

*"For my father and my mother have forsaken
me, but the Lord gathers me in."*

PSALMS 27.10

*kee a-VEE v'-i-MEE a-za-VU-nee va-do-NAI
ya-as-FAY-nee*

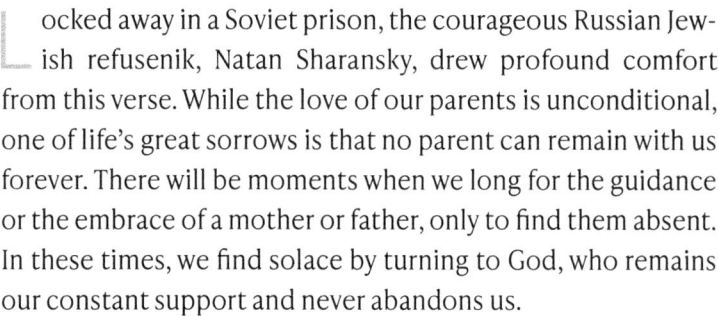

Locked away in a Soviet prison, the courageous Russian Jewish refusenik, Natan Sharansky, drew profound comfort from this verse. While the love of our parents is unconditional, one of life's great sorrows is that no parent can remain with us forever. There will be moments when we long for the guidance or the embrace of a mother or father, only to find them absent. In these times, we find solace by turning to God, who remains our constant support and never abandons us.

DATE:

Reflect on a time when you felt alone or in need of support, but were unable to turn to those you usually rely on. How did you find strength during that time? Write about how you can deepen your trust in God's unwavering presence, especially during moments when human support may fall short. How might this trust change the way you approach challenges in the future?

_____

_____

_____

_____

_____

_____

_____

_____

_____

_____

_____

_____

_____

_____

_____

_____

_____

Pray Again

"Hope for God, be strong and He will give your heart courage, and hope for God."

PSALMS 27:14

ka-VAY el a-do-NAI kha-ZAK v'-ya-a-MAYTZ li-BE-kha v'-ka-VAY el a-do-NAI

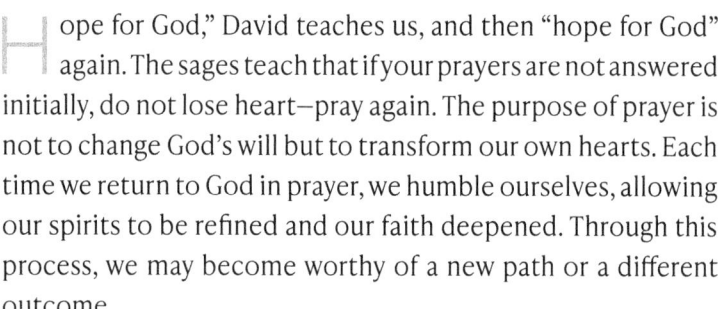

ope for God," David teaches us, and then "hope for God" again. The sages teach that if your prayers are not answered initially, do not lose heart—pray again. The purpose of prayer is not to change God's will but to transform our own hearts. Each time we return to God in prayer, we humble ourselves, allowing our spirits to be refined and our faith deepened. Through this process, we may become worthy of a new path or a different outcome.

Reflect on a time when you felt your prayers were unanswered. How did that experience affect your faith? Consider how repeated prayer could transform your understanding of the situation. Write about how you can cultivate perseverance in prayer, and how this persistence might change your heart and your relationship with God.

Turn Pain into Praise

"A song of David, to make remembrance."

PSALMS 38:1

miz-MOR l'-da-VID l'-haz-KEER

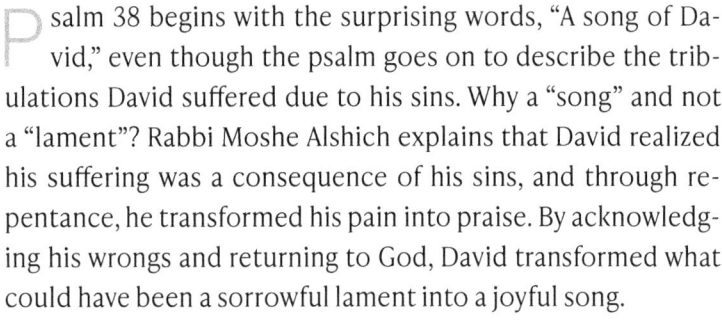

Psalm 38 begins with the surprising words, "A song of David," even though the psalm goes on to describe the tribulations David suffered due to his sins. Why a "song" and not a "lament"? Rabbi Moshe Alshich explains that David realized his suffering was a consequence of his sins, and through repentance, he transformed his pain into praise. By acknowledging his wrongs and returning to God, David transformed what could have been a sorrowful lament into a joyful song.

Reflect on a time when you faced the consequences of a mistake or sin. How did you respond to that situation? Did it lead you to despair, or were you able to find a path to repentance and renewal? How might you transform your past misdeeds into a song of praise by returning to God with a sincere heart?

Spiritual Nourishment

"Be not like a horse, like a mule that does not
discern; whose mouth must be held with bit
and bridle, so that when he is being groomed,
he does not come near you."

PSALMS 32:9

*al tih-YU k'-SUS k'-FE-red AYN ha-VEEN b'-me-teg
v'-RE-sen ed-YO liv-LOM BAL k'-ROV ay-LE-kha*

This verse warns us not to be like horses or mules who lack
understanding. These animals ignore the finest fruits and
vegetables, settling instead for dry straw. We must not make
the same mistake. God has given us the most precious gift—
His teachings in the Bible. Let us not waste our time on mean-
ingless pursuits but rather seize the opportunity to immerse
ourselves in His word, drawing close to God and finding true
nourishment for our souls.

Reflect on the ways in which you might be settling for "dry straw" in your life, ignoring the richer, more fulfilling spiritual nourishment that God offers. How can you redirect your focus toward the "delicious fruits" of God's teachings? Write about specific steps you can take to prioritize your relationship with God.

Champion Strength

"Our oxen will bear heavy loads; there is no breach nor rumor going out, nor is there a cry in our squares."

PSALMS 144:14

a-lu-FAY-nu m'-su-ba-LEEM ayn PE-retz v'-AYN yo-TZAYT v'-AYN tz'-va-KHAH bir-kho-vo-TAY-nu

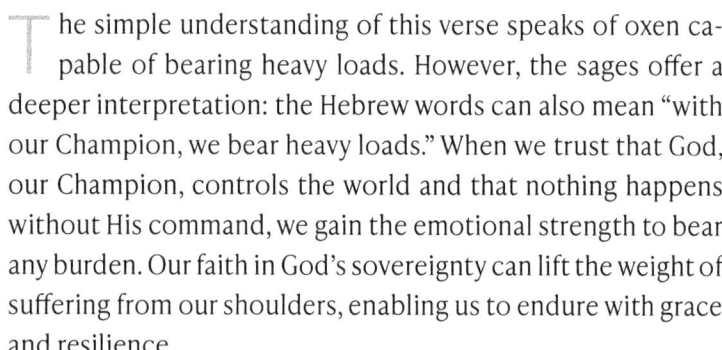

The simple understanding of this verse speaks of oxen capable of bearing heavy loads. However, the sages offer a deeper interpretation: the Hebrew words can also mean "with our Champion, we bear heavy loads." When we trust that God, our Champion, controls the world and that nothing happens without His command, we gain the emotional strength to bear any burden. Our faith in God's sovereignty can lift the weight of suffering from our shoulders, enabling us to endure with grace and resilience.

onsider a burden or challenge you are currently facing. How might your faith in God's control over the world help you bear this burden? Reflect on ways you can strengthen your trust in God and find emotional relief through that trust. Write about how embracing God as your Champion can help you endure life's challenges with greater peace and strength.

Your Personal Song

"The Lord is my strength and my shield; my heart trusted in Him and I was helped; my heart rejoiced and I will thank Him with my song."

PSALMS 28:7

a-do-NAI u-ZEE u-ma-gi-NEE BO va-TAKH li-BEE v'-ne-e-ZAR-tee va-ya-a-LOZ li-BEE u-mi-shee-REE a-ho-DE-nu

It is not enough to thank God with just any song; we must offer Him our own unique, personal song. Rabbi Kalonymus Kalman Shapira, a profound spiritual leader during the Holocaust, taught that "A person must build for himself ladders upon which to ascend to heaven, and song is one of those ladders, especially when sung... with a humble heart." Each of us has a unique melody within the "World of Melody," and it is this personal song that connects us to God in a profound way. Singing someone else's song misses the mark; we must find and express our own spiritual voice to truly connect with the Divine.

Reflect on the concept of your personal "song" in your relationship with God. What does your unique spiritual voice sound like? How can you tune into this personal melody in your prayers, worship, and daily life? Write about ways you can express your unique connection to God, ensuring that your spiritual journey is truly your own.

Sing First

"A song of David. Prepare for the Lord,
you sons of the mighty; prepare for the Lord
glory and might."

PSALMS 29:1

*miz-MOR l'-da-VID ha-VU la-do-NAI b'-NAY ay-LEEM
ha-VU la-do-NAI ka-VOD va-OZ*

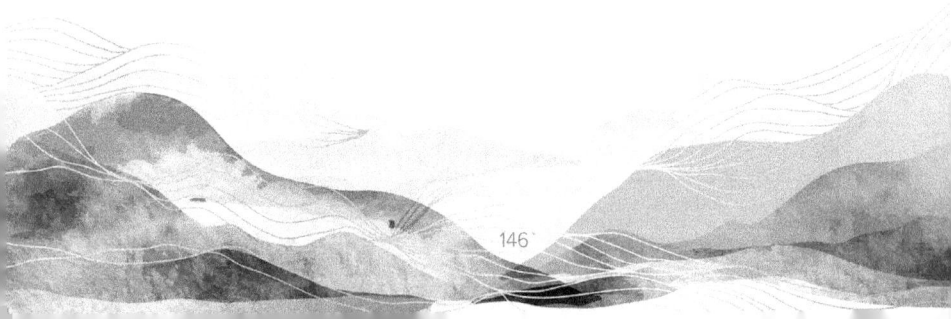

The sages teach us a profound lesson about the nature of spiritual inspiration through the opening words of the Psalms. When a psalm begins with "To David a song," it indicates that the Holy Spirit descended upon David, compelling him to sing. However, when a psalm starts with "A song of David," it means that David chose to sing first, and through his singing, the Holy Spirit then came upon him. While sometimes God's presence and inspiration come naturally and effortlessly, at other times we must actively seek Him out through song and prayer. When God feels distant, do not remain silent—sing, and He will draw near to you.

R eflect on the idea that actively seeking God through song, prayer, or other acts of devotion can bring you closer to His presence. Write about how you can incorporate this practice into your life, especially during times when you feel disconnected from God. How can you use your voice, both literally and metaphorically, to draw nearer to Him?

True Strength

"God shall grant strength to His people; God shall bless His people with peace."

PSALMS 29:11

a-do-NAI OZ l'-a-MO yi-TAYN a-do-NAI y'-va-RAYKH et a-MO va-sha-LOM

The sages teach us that the true "strength" of God's people lies not in military power, but in the Bible itself. It is this divine wisdom that has sustained the Jewish people through two millennia of exile and persecution. The Bible is also the source of "peace." Only by living according to God's will as revealed in the Bible can we achieve lasting peace in the Holy Land and in the entire world. Our ultimate strength and peace come not from human efforts but from our commitment to God's word.

R eflect on the idea that true strength and peace come from following God's will as expressed in the Bible. Consider specific areas where you can draw strength from God's word to bring peace to your relationships. Write about how you can more deeply integrate the teachings of the Bible into your daily life to find both strength and peace.

Rising Together

"I will exalt You, God, for You have raised me up, and You have not allowed my enemies to rejoice over me."

PSALMS 30:2

a-ro-mim-KHA a-do-NAI KEE di-lee-TA-nee v'-lo si-MAKH-ta o-y'-VAI LEE

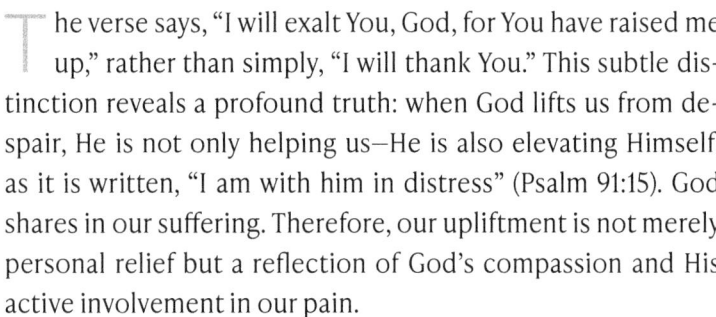

The verse says, "I will exalt You, God, for You have raised me up," rather than simply, "I will thank You." This subtle distinction reveals a profound truth: when God lifts us from despair, He is not only helping us—He is also elevating Himself, as it is written, "I am with him in distress" (Psalm 91:15). God shares in our suffering. Therefore, our upliftment is not merely personal relief but a reflection of God's compassion and His active involvement in our pain.

R eflect on the idea that God shares in our suffering. How does this perspective affect your understanding of God's involvement in your personal struggles? Write about a time when you felt uplifted from a difficult situation and consider how recognizing God's shared experience of your pain can deepen your gratitude and connection to Him. How can you express your appreciation for this divine empathy in your daily life?

According to His Will

> "For He said and it came about; He
> commanded and it endured."
>
> PSALMS 33:9

KEE HU a-MAR va-YA-hee hu tzi-VAH va-ya-a-MOD

This verse reminds us of the unimaginable power of God, who created the universe out of nothing by His word alone. Not only did He bring everything into existence, but He also continuously sustains it by His will. If God were to withhold His sustaining energy for even a moment, all creation would cease to exist. This truth humbles us, revealing that all human plans, schemes, and ambitions are insignificant compared to God's omnipotence. The Yiddish saying, "Man plans, and God laughs," captures the folly of thinking we can control our lives when, in reality, everything happens according to God's will.

Reflect on the truth that God not only created the universe but also sustains it at every moment. Consider times when your plans did not unfold as you expected, and think about how recognizing God's ultimate control might shift your response to these situations.

Ignore Evil, Do Good

"Turn away from evil and do good, seek peace
and pursue it."

PSALMS 34:15

*SUR may-RA va-a-say TOV ba-KAYSH sha-LOM
v'-rod-FAY-hu*

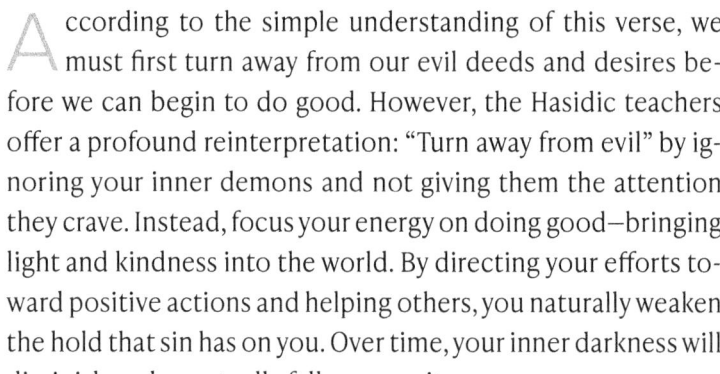

According to the simple understanding of this verse, we must first turn away from our evil deeds and desires before we can begin to do good. However, the Hasidic teachers offer a profound reinterpretation: "Turn away from evil" by ignoring your inner demons and not giving them the attention they crave. Instead, focus your energy on doing good—bringing light and kindness into the world. By directing your efforts toward positive actions and helping others, you naturally weaken the hold that sin has on you. Over time, your inner darkness will diminish and eventually fall away on its own.

dentify specific areas where you struggle with negative thoughts or behaviors, and think of positive actions you can take to counteract them. Write about how focusing on doing good for others might help you overcome these challenges and transform your inner life.

Taste the Sabbath

"Taste and see that the Lord is good;
praiseworthy is the man who takes shelter in
Him."

PSALMS 34:9

ta-a-MU ur-U kee TOV a-do-NAI ash-RAY ha-GE-ver ya-khe-seh BO

For thousands of years, traditional Jews have faithfully observed the Sabbath, adhering to its many laws and customs. On paper, keeping the Sabbath may seem overwhelming, even impossible. Many books detail the rules that make the Sabbath a uniquely holy day, but reading about it cannot convey its joy. The reality is that the true beauty and holiness of the Sabbath can only be understood through personal experience. As the Psalmist says, "Taste and see that the Lord is good." To grasp the power of the Sabbath, you must taste it for yourself—spend a Sabbath with a family or friend who observes this day, and let its peace and sanctity transform your life.

Reflect on the notion that some spiritual experiences, like the Sabbath, can only be fully understood through personal participation. How might this apply to other aspects of your spiritual journey? Write about how you might "taste and see" this aspect of your faith in a tangible way, and what you hope to gain from that experience.

Beautiful Brokenness

*"God is close to the broken-hearted,
and He saves those of crushed spirit."*

PSALMS 34:19

*ka-ROV a-do-NAI l'-nish-b'-RAY LAYV v'-et da-k'-AY
RU-akh yo-SHEE-a*

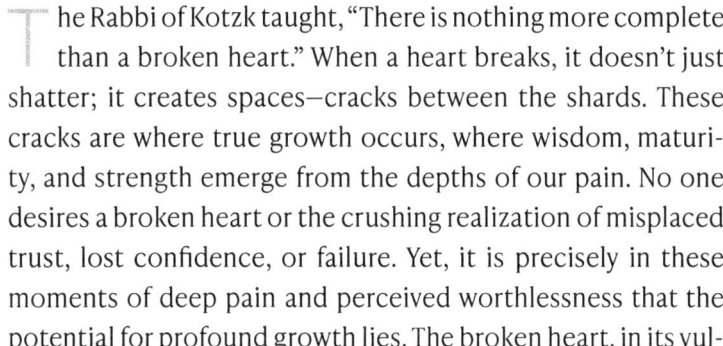

The Rabbi of Kotzk taught, "There is nothing more complete than a broken heart." When a heart breaks, it doesn't just shatter; it creates spaces—cracks between the shards. These cracks are where true growth occurs, where wisdom, maturity, and strength emerge from the depths of our pain. No one desires a broken heart or the crushing realization of misplaced trust, lost confidence, or failure. Yet, it is precisely in these moments of deep pain and perceived worthlessness that the potential for profound growth lies. The broken heart, in its vulnerability, becomes a vessel for greater transformation. "God is close to the broken-hearted."

Reflect on a time when you experienced deep emotional pain or heartbreak. How did this experience shape you? Consider the growth, wisdom, or strength that may have emerged from the cracks in your heart. In what ways did you find God's presence during this time? Write about how you can embrace the lessons learned from your brokenness and how you might approach future challenges with this understanding.

Guard Your Tongue

"Guard your tongue from evil and your lips from speaking deceitfully."

PSALMS 34:14

n'-TZOR l'-sho-n'-KHA may-RA us-fa-TE-kha mi-da-BAYR mir-MAH

The psalmist urges us to refrain from evil speech, even when the words we speak may be true. Saying that Mary is a bad driver or a terrible chef might not seem harmful, but such comments can still wound and cause hurt feelings. Words, once spoken, have a power of their own, and once they're out in the world, the damage they cause is nearly impossible to reverse. By choosing our words carefully and with kindness, we protect not only others but also the integrity of our own souls.

Think about a time when you said something that unintentionally hurt someone. How did it affect your relationship with that person? Reflect on the power of your words and how they can build up or tear down. Write about how you can commit to using your words to uplift others and create a more compassionate environment around you.

Excersice Your Heart

"He thinks iniquity on his couch; he stands on a way that is not good; he does not reject evil."

PSALMS 36.5

A-ven yakh-SHOV al mish-ka-VO yit-ya-TZAYV al DE-rekh lo TOV RA LO yim-AS

This verse warns of the subtle yet dangerous progression of sin. The Hasidic master known as the Baal Shem Tov teaches that once a person sets themselves on a path that is not good, they lose the ability to abhor evil. The heart, like any muscle, requires regular spiritual exercise to stay strong and pure. If we neglect it or allow harmful influences to take root, what was once clearly wrong can begin to seem acceptable. This moral decline often happens so gradually that we hardly notice it until it's too late.

Reflect on a time when you found yourself justifying actions or thoughts that you once knew were wrong. How did you end up on that path, and what were the consequences? Consider the small decisions you make each day and how they influence the condition of your heart. Write about how you can actively guard against the gradual erosion of your moral integrity.

Real Light

"For with You is the source of life; in Your light we will see light."

PSALMS 36:10

kee I-m'-kha m'-KOR kha-YEEM b'-o-r'-KHA nir-EH OR

True life and clarity come only from God. While the pleasures of this world may temporarily distract us, they cannot satisfy the deep spiritual thirst within us. The darkness of evil pulls us away from our true source, leaving us feeling empty and unfulfilled. It is only through the light of God that we can find real joy and insight. God's light not only guides us but also delights our souls, offering us a profound sense of purpose and fulfillment that the world alone cannot provide.

R eflect on moments when you sought fulfillment in worldly pleasures, only to find yourself still feeling empty. How has this experience shaped your understanding of true joy and contentment? Write about how you can turn more consistently toward God's light in your daily life, and the ways in which doing so might transform your spiritual thirst into lasting satisfaction.

All In

> "Commit your way to the Lord, and trust in
> Him and He will act."
>
> PSALMS 37:5

GOL al a-do-NAI dar-KE-kha uv-TAKH a-LAV v'-HU ya-a-SEH

This verse urges us to commit ourselves to the Lord. The greatest danger lies not in disbelief but in partial belief—being a "semi-believer." As C.S. Lewis observed, the most stubborn opposition often comes from those who are neither fully committed nor fully skeptical. When we half-heartedly follow God's path, we open ourselves to confusion, doubt, and bitterness. But when we fully commit ourselves to God, trusting in His wisdom and guidance, everything in life falls into place. We stop questioning what seems unfair and instead recognize that God is with us in every moment, guiding us with love and purpose.

eflect on areas in your life where you might be a "semi-believer," holding back from fully committing to God's path. How has this partial belief affected your faith, trust, and perspective on life's challenges? Write about what it would mean for you to fully commit your way to God and trust in Him without reservation. Consider specific steps you can take to strengthen your trust and fully embrace God's presence in your life.

Soul on Fire

*"My soul thirsts for God, for the living God;
when will I come and appear before God?"*

PSALMS 42:3

*tza-m'-A naf-SHEE lay-lo-HEEM l'-AYL KHAI ma-TAI
a-VO v'-ay-ra-EH p'-NAY e-lo-HEEM*

Rabbi Joseph B. Soloveitchik once observed, "True, there are Jews in America who observe the Sabbath. But it is not for the Sabbath day that my heart aches; it is for the forgotten Sabbath eve. There are Sabbath-observing Jews in America, but there are not Sabbath eve Jews here, Jews who go out to greet the Sabbath with beating hearts and pulsating souls." It is not enough to follow the rituals and laws of our faith. Our souls should burn with a deep, passionate longing for God, just as the psalmist thirsted for the living God.

Think about your own spiritual practices: Do they flow from a deep thirst for God, or have they become routine? Write about a time when you felt a profound longing for God, like the psalmist describes. How can you nurture this thirst in your daily life, ensuring that your spiritual practices are fueled by a heartfelt desire to draw closer to God?

Let It Go

*"I will recount my transgression,
anguish over my sin."*

PSALMS 38:19

KEE a-vo-NEE a-GEED ed-AG may-kha-ta-TEE

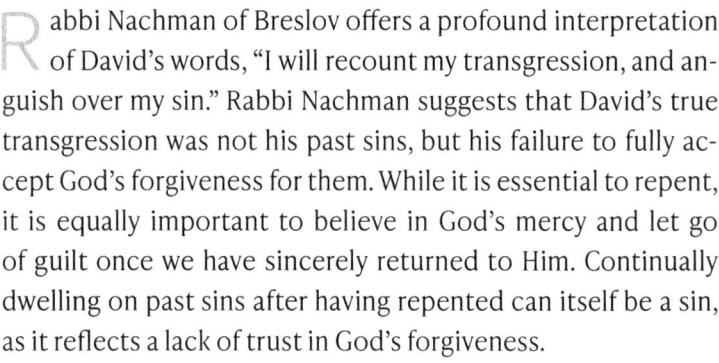

Rabbi Nachman of Breslov offers a profound interpretation of David's words, "I will recount my transgression, and anguish over my sin." Rabbi Nachman suggests that David's true transgression was not his past sins, but his failure to fully accept God's forgiveness for them. While it is essential to repent, it is equally important to believe in God's mercy and let go of guilt once we have sincerely returned to Him. Continually dwelling on past sins after having repented can itself be a sin, as it reflects a lack of trust in God's forgiveness.

R eflect on a time when you found it difficult to forgive your-self, even after seeking forgiveness from God. How might holding on to guilt impact your spiritual growth and relation-ship with God? Write about the importance of trusting in God's mercy and what steps you can take to fully embrace His forgive-ness, allowing yourself to move forward with a renewed sense of peace and purpose.

The Meaningless Chase

"Man walks but in darkness; all that they stir is but vanity; he gathers yet he knows not who will bring them in."

PSALMS 39:7

akh b'-TZE-lem yit-ha-lekh EESH akh HE-vel ye-he-ma-YUN yitz-BOR v'-lo yay-DA mee o-s'-FAM

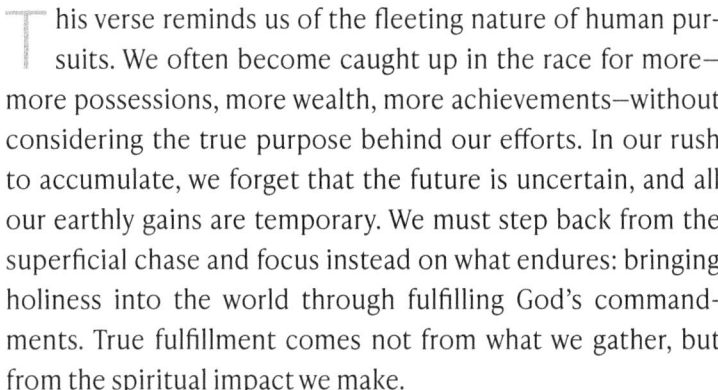

This verse reminds us of the fleeting nature of human pursuits. We often become caught up in the race for more—more possessions, more wealth, more achievements—without considering the true purpose behind our efforts. In our rush to accumulate, we forget that the future is uncertain, and all our earthly gains are temporary. We must step back from the superficial chase and focus instead on what endures: bringing holiness into the world through fulfilling God's commandments. True fulfillment comes not from what we gather, but from the spiritual impact we make.

onsider the ways in which you might be caught up in the pursuit of worldly gains. How much of your time and energy are spent on things that, in the grand scheme, may not matter? What steps can you take to ensure that your life is not wasted on vanity, but instead dedicated to bringing holiness to the world? Write about the changes you can make to prioritize what truly matters in your life.

Each Generation's Song

"He put a new song into my mouth, a praise to
our God, so that many may see and fear,
and trust in the Lord."

PSALMS 40:4

*va-yi-TAYN b'-FEE SHEER kha-DASH t'-hi-LAH lay-
lo-HAY-nu yir-U ra-BEEM v'-yee-RA-u v'-yiv-t'-KHU
ba-do-NAI*

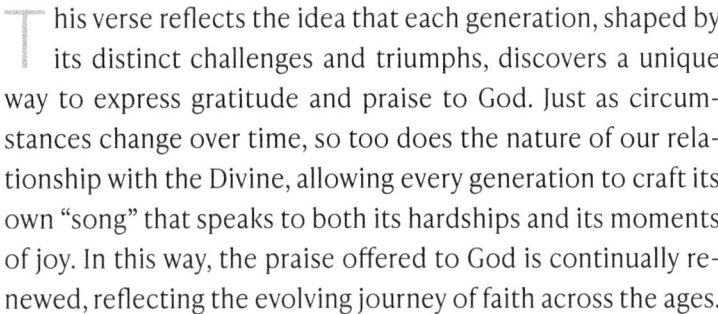

This verse reflects the idea that each generation, shaped by its distinct challenges and triumphs, discovers a unique way to express gratitude and praise to God. Just as circumstances change over time, so too does the nature of our relationship with the Divine, allowing every generation to craft its own "song" that speaks to both its hardships and its moments of joy. In this way, the praise offered to God is continually renewed, reflecting the evolving journey of faith across the ages.

W hat are the challenges and triumphs that have shaped your generation? Write about how you can use your experiences, both good and bad, to inspire a personal "new song" with which to praise God. Take a moment to think about what your "song of praise" might be—how can you give voice to your unique spiritual path and relationship with God?

Truth Will Prevail

"Praiseworthy is the man who made the Lord his trust, and did not turn to the haughty and those who turn to falsehood."

PSALMS 40:5

ASH-ray ha-GE-ver a-sher SAM a-do-NAI miv-ta-KHO v'-lo fa-NAH el r'-ha-VEEM v'-sa-TAY kha-ZAV

In a world filled with deception, where the mainstream media regularly lies to hide inconvenient truths, it is a challenge to remain steadfast in honesty. The temptation to use the tactics of falsehood, especially when it seems to offer an easier path to victory, is strong. Yet, the psalmist reminds us that true praise belongs to those who trust in God and resist the allure of arrogance and lies. The voice of the believer may seem small in a vast world of falsehood, but history has shown that it is precisely this trust in God that strengthens us and allows truth to prevail.

Consider a time when you felt pressured to compromise your values or speak falsely to achieve a goal. How did you respond? How can you remain steadfast in truth, even when it seems the world around you is filled with falsehood? Write about ways you can commit to speaking God's truth in your daily life, no matter how small your voice may seem in the larger world.

Never Alone in Pain

*"God will support him on his sickbed;
when You have transformed his entire
restfulness in his illness."*

PSALMS 41:4

*a-do-NAI yis-a-DE-nu al E-res da-VAI kol mish-ka-VO
ha-FAKH-ta v'-khol-YO*

This verse reminds us that even in the depths of illness and suffering, God is present, providing the strength and resources we need. Our Sages teach that the Divine Presence rests at the head of every sick person's bed, assuring us that God never abandons us, even in our weakest moments. The saddest experience is feeling isolated from God in times of pain, but this psalm reassures us that God is always near, offering His support and care. Even when we are at our lowest, God is close by, ready to bring us the help and comfort we need.

R eflect on a time when you or someone you love faced illness. How did you experience God's presence during that time? Consider how this psalm's message of God's closeness in times of suffering might change your perspective on your own struggles, and how you might offer that same reassurance to others in need.

Desperate for God

*"Like a hind crying for water,
my soul cries for You, O God."*

PSALMS 42:2

*k'-a-YAL ta-a-ROG al a-fee-kay MA-yim, KAYN naf-
SHEE ta-a-ROG ay-LE-kha e-lo-HEEM*

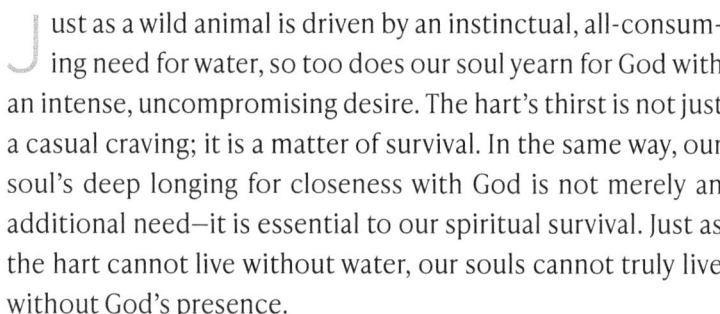

Just as a wild animal is driven by an instinctual, all-consuming need for water, so too does our soul yearn for God with an intense, uncompromising desire. The hart's thirst is not just a casual craving; it is a matter of survival. In the same way, our soul's deep longing for closeness with God is not merely an additional need—it is essential to our spiritual survival. Just as the hart cannot live without water, our souls cannot truly live without God's presence.

Reflect on a time when you felt a deep longing for spiritual connection or a sense of closeness with God. What circumstances in your life increased this desire, and how did you seek to fulfill it? Write about ways you can nurture this deep yearning for God and allow it to guide your actions and choices.

True Security

> "For not by their sword did they inherit the land, neither did their arm save them, but Your right hand and Your arm and the light of Your countenance, for You favored them."

PSALMS 44:4

kee LO v'-khar-BAM ya-r'-SHU A-retz uz-ro-AM lo ho-SHEE-ah LA-mo kee y'-mee-n'-KHA uz-ro-a-KHA v'-OR pa-NE-kha kee r'-tzee-TAM

Israel's victories were never due to their military might or alliances with powerful nations. Rather, it was God's intervention, favor, and guiding presence that secured their inheritance. Our true security does not come from worldly powers or our own efforts, but from trusting in God's providence and guidance.

Are there areas in your life where you place too much trust in worldly sources of security—whether it be finances, relationships, or personal abilities? How can you shift your reliance from these external sources to trusting more fully in God's power and favor? Has there been a time when you experienced God's guidance or intervention in a situation where human efforts fell short? Consider how this can shape your trust in Him going forward.

False Friends

"Avenge me, O God, and plead my cause against an unkind nation, from a man of deceit and injustice You shall rescue me."

PSALMS 43:1

sha-f'-TAY-nee e-lo-HEEM v'-REE-vah ree-VEE mi-GOY lo kha-SEED may-EESH mir-MAH v'-av-LAH t'-fal-TAY-nee

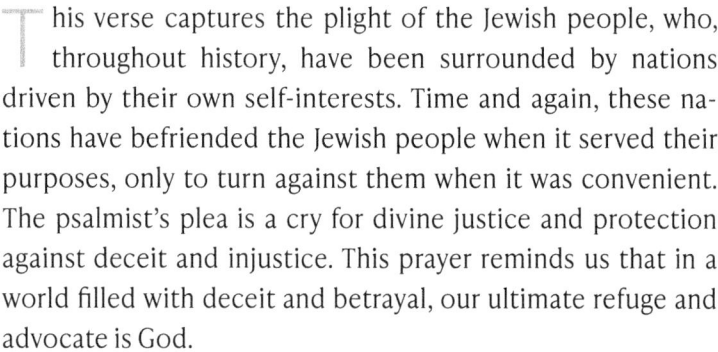

This verse captures the plight of the Jewish people, who, throughout history, have been surrounded by nations driven by their own self-interests. Time and again, these nations have befriended the Jewish people when it served their purposes, only to turn against them when it was convenient. The psalmist's plea is a cry for divine justice and protection against deceit and injustice. This prayer reminds us that in a world filled with deceit and betrayal, our ultimate refuge and advocate is God.

Reflect on times when you or your community felt vulnerable or betrayed by those you trusted. How did you seek God's protection and justice in those moments? How can you draw strength from this verse in trusting God as your defender against the world's unkindness?

God's Enduring Covenant

"O God, with our ears we heard, our forefathers told us; You performed a deed in their days, in days of old."

PSALMS 44:2

e-lo-HEEM b'-oz-NAY-nu sha-MA-nu a-vo-TAY-nu si-p'-ru LA-nu PO-al pa-AL-ta vee-may-HEM bee-MAY KE-dem

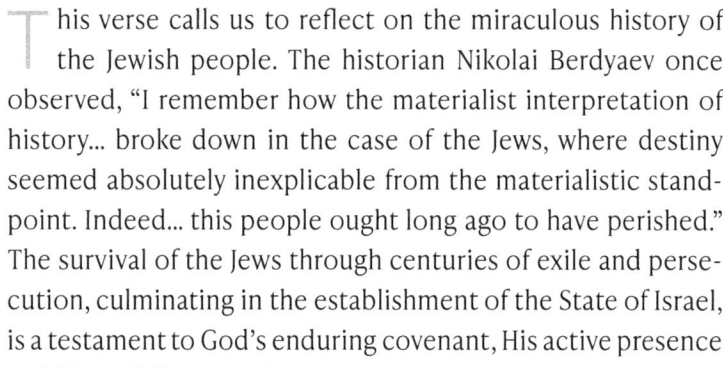

This verse calls us to reflect on the miraculous history of the Jewish people. The historian Nikolai Berdyaev once observed, "I remember how the materialist interpretation of history... broke down in the case of the Jews, where destiny seemed absolutely inexplicable from the materialistic standpoint. Indeed... this people ought long ago to have perished." The survival of the Jews through centuries of exile and persecution, culminating in the establishment of the State of Israel, is a testament to God's enduring covenant, His active presence and His unfailing promises.

Reflect on the miraculous survival and resilience of the Jewish people throughout history. How does the enduring existence of the Jewish people, despite centuries of exile and persecution, strengthen your faith in God's covenant and promises? Consider how this history might inspire you in your own life, especially during times of challenge or uncertainty. What lessons of faith, perseverance, and divine purpose can you draw from this legacy?

Get Back Up

"If he falls, he will not be cast down, for the
Lord supports his hand."

PSALMS 37:24

kee yi-POL lo yu-TAL kee a-do-NAI so-MAYKH ya-DO

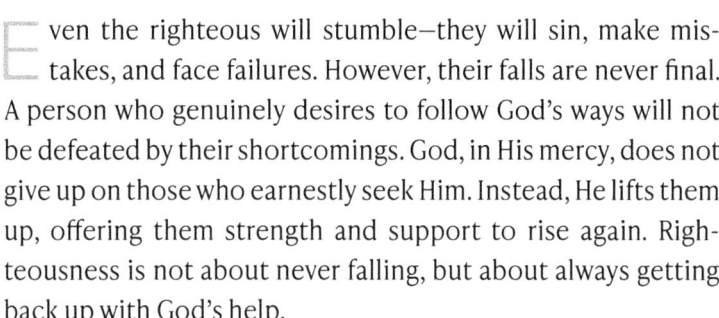

Even the righteous will stumble—they will sin, make mistakes, and face failures. However, their falls are never final. A person who genuinely desires to follow God's ways will not be defeated by their shortcomings. God, in His mercy, does not give up on those who earnestly seek Him. Instead, He lifts them up, offering them strength and support to rise again. Righteousness is not about never falling, but about always getting back up with God's help.

Reflect on a time when you fell short or failed in your spiritual journey. How did you find the strength to rise again? How does knowing that God upholds you, even when you stumble, change the way you view your own imperfections? Write about an area in your life where you feel you've fallen but want to get back on track.

Humble Inheritance

"But the humble shall inherit the land, and they shall delight in much peace."

PSALMS 37:11

va-a-na-VEEM yee-r'-shu A-retz v'-hit-a-n'-GU al ROV sha-LOM

The ultimate claim to the Land of Israel is not through military might or human power alone, but through humility and righteousness. While the courage and sacrifice of the IDF are necessary to protect the land, we must also recognize that the land belongs to God. Our connection to it is spiritual as well as physical, and it is through living according to God's ways that we earn the right to dwell in the land. True inheritance comes not from dominance, but from understanding our role as stewards of God's creation, living with humility and a deep sense of purpose.

Reflect on a time when humility allowed you to achieve something that force or pride could not. What steps can you take to ensure that your actions are aligned with God's will, and that you approach challenges with a spirit of humility rather than a desire for power? In what ways can you cultivate humility in your own life, and how might that strengthen your relationship with God and the Land of Israel?

Look Beyond the Moment

"I was young, I also aged, and I have not seen a righteous man forsaken and his seed seeking bread."

PSALMS 37:25

*NA-ar ha-YEE-tee gam za-KAN-tee v'-lo ra-EE-tee
tza-DEEK ne-e-ZAV v'-zar-O m'-va-kesh LA-khem*

This verse seems naive, as we know that many righteous people do suffer and struggle to find enough to eat. However, the psalmist is encouraging us to take a long-term view of life. While immediate circumstances might suggest that the righteous are abandoned, we must look beyond the moment. Over the course of generations, we can see that God does not forsake the righteous. Their legacy, their influence, and often their descendants are blessed and sustained. This perspective challenges us to trust in God's long-term plan, even when the present is difficult.

Reflect on how adopting a long-term view might help you better trust in God's plan for your life. How can you cultivate patience and faith when the rewards of righteousness aren't immediately visible?

See Truth

"The Lord gives sight to the blind;
the Lord straightens the bent;
the Lord loves the righteous."

PSALMS 146:8

*a-do-NAI po-KAY-akh iv-REEM a-do-NAI zo-KAYF
k'-fu-FEEM a-do-NAI o-HAYV tza-dee-KEEM*

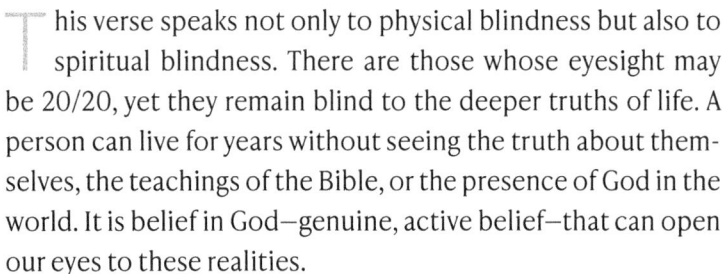

This verse speaks not only to physical blindness but also to spiritual blindness. There are those whose eyesight may be 20/20, yet they remain blind to the deeper truths of life. A person can live for years without seeing the truth about themselves, the teachings of the Bible, or the presence of God in the world. It is belief in God—genuine, active belief—that can open our eyes to these realities.

R eflect on areas in your life where you may have been "blind" to the truth, whether about yourself, your relationships, or your understanding of God. How has your faith helped you see more clearly? Consider where you still might be missing important insights and how you can cultivate a deeper, more active faith to help reveal those truths.

Sacred Souls

"Hallelujah! My soul, praise the Lord."

PSALMS 146:1

ha-l'-lu-YAH ha-l'-LEE naf-SHEE et a-do-NAI

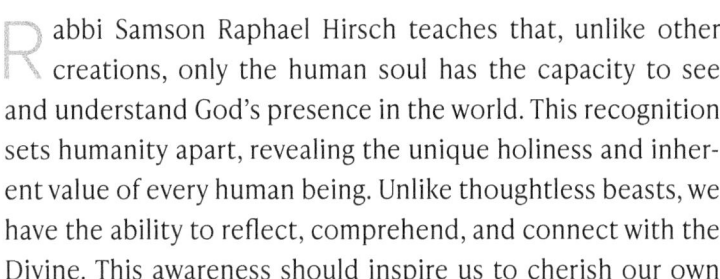

Rabbi Samson Raphael Hirsch teaches that, unlike other creations, only the human soul has the capacity to see and understand God's presence in the world. This recognition sets humanity apart, revealing the unique holiness and inherent value of every human being. Unlike thoughtless beasts, we have the ability to reflect, comprehend, and connect with the Divine. This awareness should inspire us to cherish our own souls and the souls of others, recognizing the profound dignity that comes with being able to know God.

C onsider the unique capacity you have as a human being to recognize and connect with God. How does this awareness influence the way you see yourself and others? Write about how acknowledging the unique value of every human soul can shape your actions and relationships.

Always Thankful

"I shall praise the Lord in my life;
I shall sing to the Lord as long as I exist."

PSALMS 146:2

a-ha-l'-LAH a-do-NAI b'-kha-YAI a-za-m'-RAH lay-lo-HAI b'-o-DEE

Rabbi Meir Wisser suggests that this verse can also be read as, "I will praise God for the fact that I am alive and I will sing praises for the fact that He also watches over me." This perspective encourages us to recognize that, regardless of our circumstances, we always have reasons to be thankful. The very fact we are alive is a gift from God, and His continual care and protection are further reasons to sing His praises. By focusing on these fundamental blessings, we can cultivate gratitude no matter what life brings.

R eflect on the simple yet profound blessings of life and God's watchful care over you. Write about how you can cultivate a habit of praising God, not just for extraordinary blessings, but for the everyday miracle of being alive and under His protection.

Divine Prescriptions

"God is righteous in all His ways
and kind in all His deeds."

PSALMS 145:17

*tza-DEEK a-do-NAI b'-khol d'-ra-KHAV v'-kha-SEED
b'-khol ma-a-SAV*

I f God is righteous, why do some people live in wealth and ease while others struggle for their daily bread? Rabbi Abraham ibn Ezra explains that God's righteousness is like that of a skilled doctor who prescribes different treatments for different patients. Just as a doctor gives each person the medicine they uniquely need, God provides each of us with what is most necessary for our spiritual and personal growth. What may seem unfair or uneven in our eyes is, in fact, tailored to help each person fulfill their purpose and potential.

R eflect on a time when you questioned why others seemed to have more or less than you. How does the idea that God gives each person what they need for their unique journey change your perspective? Consider your own life—what might God be trying to teach or develop in you through your current circumstances?

Beyond Words

"Praise Him with His mighty deeds, praise Him as befits His superb greatness."

PSALMS 150:2

ha-l'-LU-hu vig-vu-ro-TAV ha-l'-LU-hu k'-ROV gud-LO

There are moments when words fall short of capturing the full scope of God's magnificence. There are times when we encounter something so awe-inspiring—whether a breathtaking landscape, a profound moment of connection, or a deeply moving experience—that words alone cannot fully convey our feelings. In such moments, music and song transcend the limitations of language to reflect the depth of our admiration and wonder.

Think of a time when you experienced something so profound or beautiful that words felt inadequate. Reflect on how these moments influence your ability to praise God. How can you use creative expressions like music or art to enhance your spiritual practice and deepen your connection to the divine?

Known by Name

"He counts the number of the stars; He calls them all by name."

PSALMS 147:4

mo-NEH mis-PAR la-ko-kha-VEEM l'-khu-LAM shay-MOT yik-RA

According to the sages, every person has a star in the heavens that corresponds to them, shining according to their actions. Just as God knows the name of every star, He also knows the name of every one of His creations, including you. This teaching reminds us of God's intimate knowledge and care for each individual. We are not lost in the vastness of the universe; we are known and cherished by the Creator Himself.

R eflect on the idea that God knows and cares for you personally, just as He knows each star by name. How does this impact your sense of worth and purpose? Consider moments in your life when you've felt particularly seen or known by God. How can you strengthen your awareness of His personal care in your daily life?

Sacred Weather

"He gives snow like wool;
He scatters hoarfrost like ashes."

PSALMS 147:16

*ha-no-TAYN SHE-leg ka-TZA-mer k'-FOR ka-AY-fer
y'-fa-ZAYR*

In today's world, it's easy to view the weather as merely the outcome of scientific forces, complex and often unpredictable. However, the psalmist reminds us that God is the ultimate force behind all of nature. The cycles of weather, from snow to frost, are under His control and serve His purposes. A truly religious person recognizes God's hand in the natural world, understanding that even the weather—whether it brings blessings or challenges—reflects His will and care for creation.

R eflect on a time when you experienced the power of nature, whether through a beautiful day or a challenging storm. How did it make you feel, and how often do you stop to consider God's presence in the natural world around you? Consider how viewing the weather and nature as part of God's will might change your perspective on both everyday moments and larger challenges.

Fresh Praise Daily

"Hallelujah! Sing to the Lord a new song; His praise is in the congregation of the pious."

PSALMS 149:1

*ha-l'-lu-YAH shee-RU la-do-NAI SHEER kha-DASH
t'-hi-la-TO bik-HAL kha-see-DEEM*

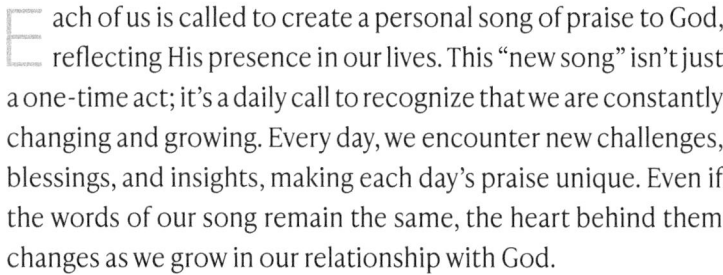

Each of us is called to create a personal song of praise to God, reflecting His presence in our lives. This "new song" isn't just a one-time act; it's a daily call to recognize that we are constantly changing and growing. Every day, we encounter new challenges, blessings, and insights, making each day's praise unique. Even if the words of our song remain the same, the heart behind them changes as we grow in our relationship with God.

Reflect on how you have changed over the past day, week, or month. How have your experiences, challenges, and growth in faith shaped your relationship with God? Write a "new song" of praise, acknowledging how God's presence has been active in your life recently.

The Gateway to Heaven

"Ascribe to the Lord the glory due His name; carry an offering and come to His courtyards."

PSALMS 96.8

ha-VU la-do-NAI k'-VOD sh'-MO s'-u min-KHAH u-VO-u l'-khatz-ro-TAV

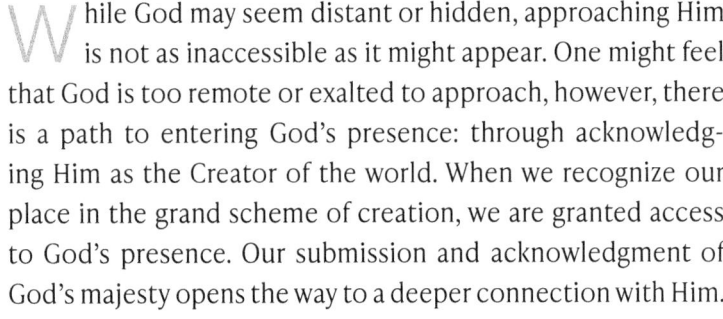

While God may seem distant or hidden, approaching Him is not as inaccessible as it might appear. One might feel that God is too remote or exalted to approach, however, there is a path to entering God's presence: through acknowledging Him as the Creator of the world. When we recognize our place in the grand scheme of creation, we are granted access to God's presence. Our submission and acknowledgment of God's majesty opens the way to a deeper connection with Him.

Reflect on moments when God has seemed distant or unreachable in your life. How might acknowledging God's role as the Creator and recognizing your place within His creation help you feel closer to Him? Consider how humility and submission to God's majesty can open the door to a deeper connection. What steps can you take to actively cultivate this sense of closeness to God?

Enter with Joy

"Come, let us sing praises to the Lord; let us shout to the rock of our salvation."

PSALMS 95:1

l'-KHU n'-ra-n'-NAH la-do-NAI na-REE-ah l'-TZUR yish-AY-nu

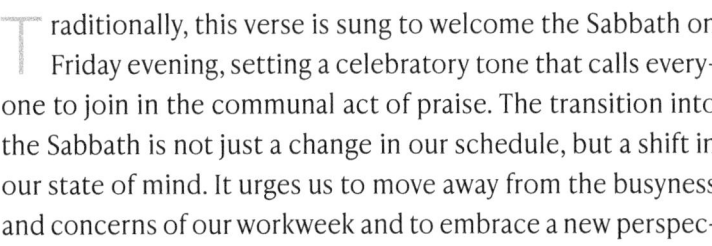

Traditionally, this verse is sung to welcome the Sabbath on Friday evening, setting a celebratory tone that calls everyone to join in the communal act of praise. The transition into the Sabbath is not just a change in our schedule, but a shift in our state of mind. It urges us to move away from the busyness and concerns of our workweek and to embrace a new perspective of rest and spiritual renewal. By singing and shouting with joy, we actively prepare ourselves to enter into a different, more sacred space.

C onsider how you prepare for the special spiritual practices in your life. Reflect on how you shift your mindset from the demands of everyday life to a state of spiritual awareness and rest. What practices or rituals help you make this transition effectively?

Modern Miracles

"Do not harden your heart as in Meribah, as on the day of Massah in the desert."

PSALMS 95.8

al tak-SHU l'-vav-KHEM kim-ree-VAH k'-YOM ma-SAH ba-mid-BAR

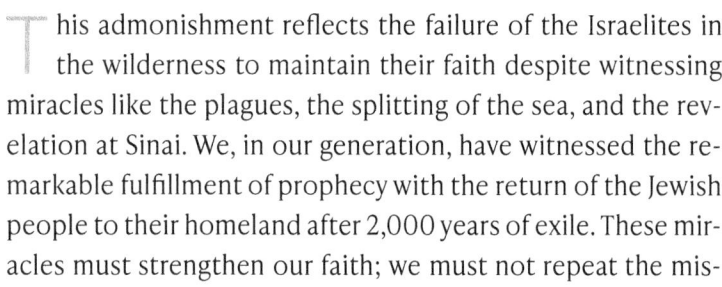

This admonishment reflects the failure of the Israelites in the wilderness to maintain their faith despite witnessing miracles like the plagues, the splitting of the sea, and the revelation at Sinai. We, in our generation, have witnessed the remarkable fulfillment of prophecy with the return of the Jewish people to their homeland after 2,000 years of exile. These miracles must strengthen our faith; we must not repeat the mistakes of the past.

Reflect on the modern-day miracles you've witnessed, such as the return of the Jewish people to their homeland, and how they have impacted your faith. Consider whether there are areas in your life where you struggle to maintain faith despite the signs of God's presence. How can you use the lessons from the past to strengthen your belief and avoid repeating the same mistakes?

True Wealth

"Fear the Lord, His holy ones; for there is no want to those who fear Him."

PSALMS 34:10

y'-r'-U et a-do-NAI k'-do-SHAV, kee AYN makh-SOR lee-ray-AV

T he sages teach, "Who is wealthy? The person who is happy with what he has." This verse does not promise material riches to those who fear God, but rather assures that they will lack nothing essential. True wealth is not measured by the abundance of possessions but by contentment with what we have. Envy of others' material wealth is futile; satisfaction comes from appreciating and valuing our own blessings.

Reflect on your own sense of contentment. How do you feel about what you currently have in terms of material possessions, relationships, and achievements? How can you cultivate a greater sense of gratitude and contentment in your daily life?

Radiate Joy

"Ascribe to the Lord, you families of nations,
ascribe to the Lord glory and might."

PSALMS 96:7

*ha-VU la-do-NAI mish-p'-KHOT a-MIM ha-VU la-do-
NAI ka-VOD va-OZ*

The greatest gift that the people of Israel gave the world is the understanding that there is one God who is sovereign over all creation.Standing in the presence of God brings immense joy and fulfillment, and we naturally desire to share the goodness of God with others. Jews share their faith not by proselytizing or imposing their will but by radiating their happiness to others. This approach invites others to experience the same joy and connection with God, encouraging them to explore and embrace the divine presence in their own lives.

Consider how you can embody and express your joy in a way that inspires and uplifts those around you, without imposing your beliefs. How can your own joyful relationship with God serve as an example to others?

Sabbath Clarity

"All worshippers of graven images will be ashamed, yea those who boast of idols; all gods, prostrate yourselves before Him."

PSALMS 97:7

yay-VO-shu kol OV-day FE-sel ha-mit-ha-l'-LEEM ba-e-lee-LEEM hish-ta-kha-vu LO kol e-lo-HEEM

This verse can also be translated as, "Those who worship images and are praised through idols will be put to shame." People rejoice in their gods - idols, money, materialism, career success and fame - but in our heart of hearts we know that what really counts is to be a good person. We recite this verse on the Sabbath, for the Sabbath is a weekly opportunity to realign our priorities. By stepping away from the distractions and pursuits of everyday life, we can regain a clearer perspective on what truly matters.

Consider the things or achievements in your life that you may have placed on a pedestal, whether they be material possessions, career accomplishments, or social status. Reflect on how these idols have influenced your happiness and sense of self-worth. How can the perspective you gain from the Sabbath help you shift your focus from fleeting idols to lasting values?

Transcendent Yet Present

"The Lord is great in Zion, and He is high over all the peoples."

PSALMS 99:2

a-do-NAI b'-tzee-YON ga-DOL v'-RAM HU al kol ha-a-MEEM

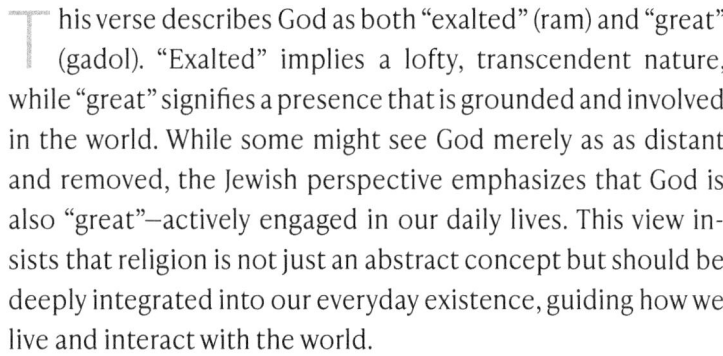

This verse describes God as both "exalted" (ram) and "great" (gadol). "Exalted" implies a lofty, transcendent nature, while "great" signifies a presence that is grounded and involved in the world. While some might see God merely as as distant and removed, the Jewish perspective emphasizes that God is also "great"—actively engaged in our daily lives. This view insists that religion is not just an abstract concept but should be deeply integrated into our everyday existence, guiding how we live and interact with the world.

D o you view God as distant and exalted, or do you also see Him as "great," involved in your personal experiences and challenges? How does your understanding of God's role influence your approach to your daily activities, relationships, and spiritual practices? Write about how recognizing God's involvement in your daily life might change the way you relate to the world around you.

Crack Open Your Heart

"Shout for joy to the Lord, all the earth, burst into song, sing with joy, play music."

PSALMS 98:4

ha-REE-u la-do-NAI kol ha-A-retz pitz-KHU v'-ra-n'-NU v'-za-MAY-ru

In Hebrew, the word "burst" (pitzchu) can mean to burst or to crack open. Sometimes, we don't feel inspired or in the mood to sing, and we must "crack open" our hearts to let our inner voice and true feelings emerge. Genuine expression of praise to God does not always come easily. It often involves overcoming our initial resistance to fully opening up our hearts.

Reflect on a time when you had to push past your initial resistance or reluctance to fully express yourself, whether through singing, sharing your thoughts, or showing your emotions. What did you learn from the experience about the importance of opening yourself up and being vulnerable?

Nature's Voice

"The voice of the Lord is in strength; the voice of the Lord is in beauty."

PSALMS 29:4

kol a-do-NAI ba-KO-akh kol a-do-NAI be-ha-DAR

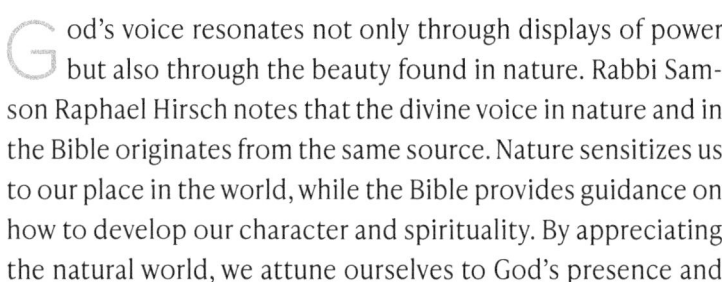

God's voice resonates not only through displays of power but also through the beauty found in nature. Rabbi Samson Raphael Hirsch notes that the divine voice in nature and in the Bible originates from the same source. Nature sensitizes us to our place in the world, while the Bible provides guidance on how to develop our character and spirituality. By appreciating the natural world, we attune ourselves to God's presence and deepen our understanding of His teachings.

Reflect on an experience in nature that deeply moved you. How did the beauty of the natural world impact your thoughts, feelings, or sense of purpose? How does experiencing the beauty of nature make you feel more attuned to God's presence? How might that experience inform your understanding of God's teachings in the Bible and enhance your spiritual development?

Sabbath Vision

"When the wicked flourish like grass, and all workers of violence blossom, only to be destroyed to eternity."

PSALMS 92:8

bif-RO-akh r'-sha-EEM k'-mo AY-sev va-ya-TZEE-tzu kol po-a-LAY A-ven l'-hi-sha-m'-DAM a-day AD

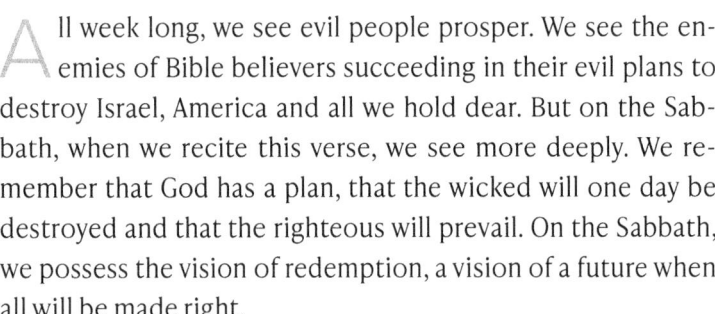

All week long, we see evil people prosper. We see the enemies of Bible believers succeeding in their evil plans to destroy Israel, America and all we hold dear. But on the Sabbath, when we recite this verse, we see more deeply. We remember that God has a plan, that the wicked will one day be destroyed and that the righteous will prevail. On the Sabbath, we possess the vision of redemption, a vision of a future when all will be made right.

Reflect on moments when you have observed apparent prosperity of those who act against your values. How does the message of the Sabbath help you realign your focus on God's plan and the ultimate triumph of good over evil?

Lasting Treasures

"They are to be desired more than gold, yea more than much fine gold, and are sweeter than honey and drippings of honeycombs."

PSALMS 19:11

ha-ne-khe-ma-DEEM mi-za-HAV u-mi-PAZ RAV
um-tu-KEEM mi-d'-VASH v'-NO-fet tzu-FEEM

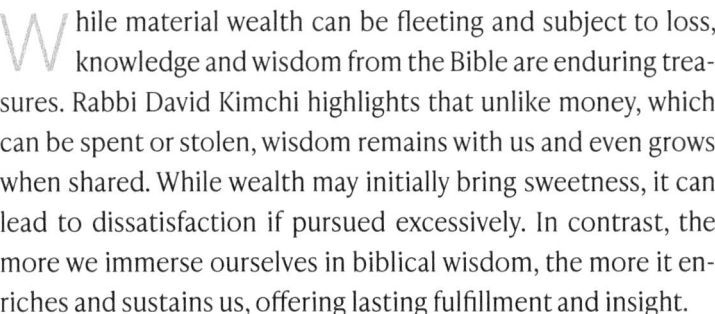

While material wealth can be fleeting and subject to loss, knowledge and wisdom from the Bible are enduring treasures. Rabbi David Kimchi highlights that unlike money, which can be spent or stolen, wisdom remains with us and even grows when shared. While wealth may initially bring sweetness, it can lead to dissatisfaction if pursued excessively. In contrast, the more we immerse ourselves in biblical wisdom, the more it enriches and sustains us, offering lasting fulfillment and insight.

Reflect on the value of wisdom compared to material wealth. How has your understanding of biblical teachings enhanced your sense of fulfillment? Consider a recent experience where sharing knowledge or wisdom has positively impacted you or others.

Born for This

"I will bless the Lord at all times;
His praise is always in my mouth."

PSALMS 34:2

a-va-r'-KHAH et a-do-NAI b'-khol AYT, ta-MEED t'-hi-la-TO b'-FEE

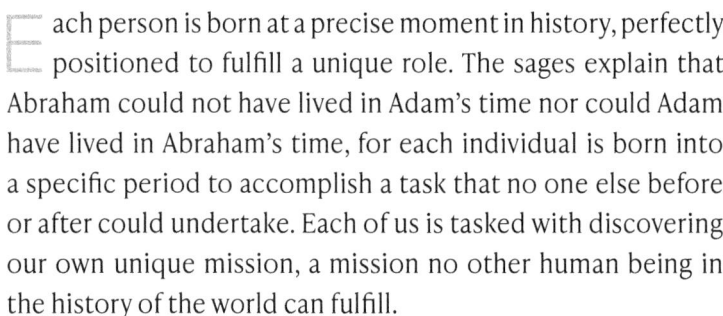

Each person is born at a precise moment in history, perfectly positioned to fulfill a unique role. The sages explain that Abraham could not have lived in Adam's time nor could Adam have lived in Abraham's time, for each individual is born into a specific period to accomplish a task that no one else before or after could undertake. Each of us is tasked with discovering our own unique mission, a mission no other human being in the history of the world can fulfill.

Consider your place in history and reflect on what you believe your unique role might be. Write about a moment or opportunity where you felt particularly aligned with your purpose, and how this awareness influences your actions and goals.

Wilderness Wisdom

"To Him Who led His people in the desert, for His kindness is eternal."

PSALMS 136:16

l'-mo-LEEKH a-MO ba-mid-BAR, KEE l'-o-LAM khas-DO

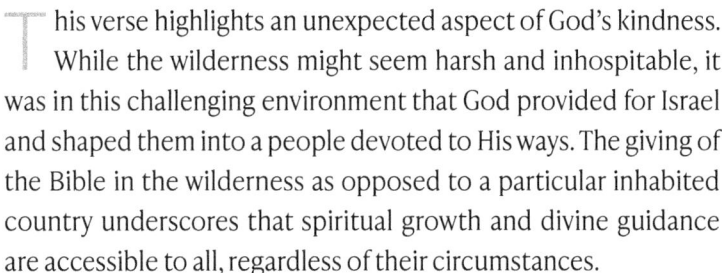

This verse highlights an unexpected aspect of God's kindness. While the wilderness might seem harsh and inhospitable, it was in this challenging environment that God provided for Israel and shaped them into a people devoted to His ways. The giving of the Bible in the wilderness as opposed to a particular inhabited country underscores that spiritual growth and divine guidance are accessible to all, regardless of their circumstances.

How does the leading the Israelites through the desert reflect God's kindness? Think about a time in your life when you were going through a "wilderness" season. In what ways did that challenging environment shape your character or deepen your faith? How might this perspective encourage you to see difficult times as opportunities for divine guidance and growth?

Return Together

"You bring man to the crushing point,
and You say, 'Return, O sons of men.'"

PSALMS 90:3

*ta-SHAYV e-NOSH ad da-KA, va-TO-mer SHU-vu
v'-nay a-DAM*

The verse uses the plural form, "return, O sons of men," highlighting the communal aspect of spiritual renewal. It teaches us that sometimes we cannot overcome sadness or sin on our own; we need the support and kindness of others to help us return to our true, holy selves. Worship and spiritual growth are not meant to be solitary endeavors. By surrounding ourselves with friends who are also dedicated to serving God, we create an environment where we can support and strengthen one another in our pursuit of holiness.

Consider the role that community plays in your spiritual journey. Reflect on times when the support of friends or a community has helped you overcome challenges or grow in your faith. How can you actively seek to surround yourself with people who share your commitment to serving God?

Chase Peace

"Shun evil and do good,
seek peace and pursue it."

PSALMS 34:15

SUR may-RA va-a-say TOV, ba-KAYSH sha-LOM
v'-rod-FAY-hu

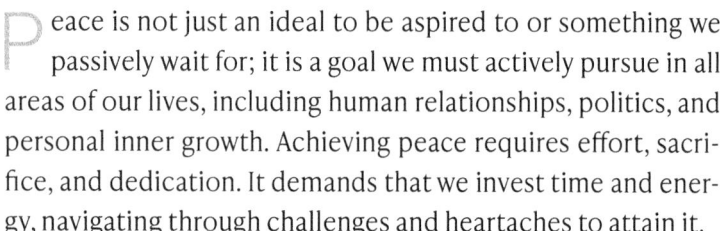

Peace is not just an ideal to be aspired to or something we passively wait for; it is a goal we must actively pursue in all areas of our lives, including human relationships, politics, and personal inner growth. Achieving peace requires effort, sacrifice, and dedication. It demands that we invest time and energy, navigating through challenges and heartaches to attain it.

R eflect on areas in your life where you can actively work towards peace. What steps can you take to pursue peace in these areas? Write about the sacrifices and efforts you are willing to make to achieve peace and how this pursuit could positively impact the lives of those around you.

Stay Awake

"You carry them away as a flood; they are like a sleep; in the morning, like grass it passes away."

PSALMS 90:5

z'-ram-TAM shay-NAH yi-h'-YU, ba-BO-ker ke-kha-TZEER ya-kha-LOF

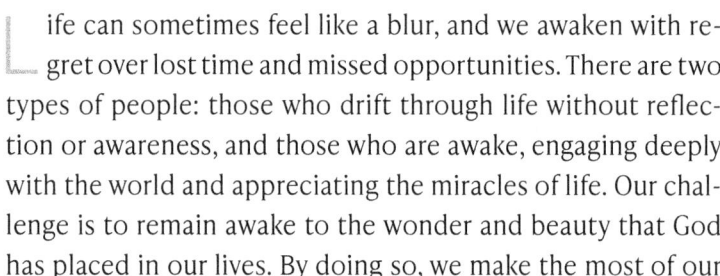

Life can sometimes feel like a blur, and we awaken with regret over lost time and missed opportunities. There are two types of people: those who drift through life without reflection or awareness, and those who are awake, engaging deeply with the world and appreciating the miracles of life. Our challenge is to remain awake to the wonder and beauty that God has placed in our lives. By doing so, we make the most of our time and embrace the full richness of life.

Consider the ways you might be sleepwalking through life. Reflect on moments when you felt disconnected or unengaged with your surroundings and opportunities. How can you become more present and mindful in your daily life?

Live Today

"Return, O Lord, how long?
And repent about Your servants."

PSALMS 90:13

*shu-VAH a-do-NAI ad ma-TAI, v'-hi-na-KHAYM al
a-va-DE-kha*

The sages understand this verse as a call for man to repent on the day before he dies. Since the exact day of our death is unknown, we must repent every day of our lives with a sense of urgency and reflection. By living each day as though it could be our final one, we cultivate a habit of repentance and spiritual readiness, ensuring that we remain aligned with our values and purpose.

Reflect on how you would live if you knew today were your last day. What would you change in your daily routine, relationships, or personal goals? How can you ensure that you live every day with purpose and integrity?

_____

_____

_____

_____

_____

_____

_____

_____

_____

_____

_____

_____

_____

_____

_____

_____

_____

_____

_____

Present in Pain

"He will call Me and I shall answer him;
I am with him in distress; I shall rescue him
and I shall honor him."

PSALMS 91:15

yik-ra-AY-nee v'-e-e-NAY-hu i-MO a-no-KHEE v'-tza-
RAH, a-kha-l'-TZAY-hu va-a-kha-b'-DAY-hu

According to the sages, when Moses questioned why God chose to reveal Himself at the burning bush from a lowly thornbush rather than a grander tree, God responded, "My people are suffering as slaves in Egypt, and I should reveal Myself from a more exalted tree?" In this conversation, God emphasizes that He is with His people in their suffering, sharing in their distress. God's presence is most profoundly felt in our moments of pain. He is not distant or removed, but feels our pain together with us.

How does the image of God standing with us in times of pain resonate with your own experiences? Have you ever felt God's presence more strongly during moments of struggle or hardship? How might this understanding shape the way you approach difficult situations in your life?

Words Create Worlds

"By the word of the Lord, the heavens were made, and with the breath of His mouth, all their host."

PSALMS 33:6

bid-VAR a-do-NAI sha-MA-yim na-a-SU, uv-RU-akh PEEV kol tz'-va-AM

In this verse we read of the profound power of divine speech in creation: "By the word of the Lord the heavens were made." Just as God brought the world into existence through His utterance, our own words possess transformative power. The sages teach that speech is akin to action; our words can build and uplift or tear down and destroy. We are called to speak with intention and mindfulness, recognizing that our words can shape our world and impact others profoundly.

DATE:

Reflect on a time when your words had a significant impact—either positively or negatively. Consider the ways you can use your words intentionally to create positive change and build up those around you. How can you become more mindful of the impact your speech has on your relationships and your environment?

Prepare for Prayer

*"Fortunate are those who stay in Your house;
they will continually praise You forever."*

PSALMS 84.5

*ash-RAY yo-sh'-VAY vay-TE-kha OD y'-ha-l'-LU-kha
SE-lah*

The verse speaks of those who are fortunate to "dwell" in God's house. But who are these fortunate "dwellers?" The Sages explain that true, heartfelt prayer requires mental preparation. "One should not rise to pray until first acquiring a reverent state of mind." It requires mental effort to transition from our daily concerns to a focused, reverent mindset. "Dwelling" in God's house represents the preparatory step of calming and clearing our minds in preparation for prayer.

C onsider how you prepare yourself for prayer or spiritual practice. Reflect on ways you can create a more intentional and mindful approach to your spiritual routines, ensuring that you're fully present and engaged in your moments of prayer and reflection.

Sacred Trust

"The heavens are heavens of the Lord, but the earth He gave to the children of men."

PSALMS 115.16

ha-sha-MA-yim sha-MA-yim la-do-NAI, v'-ha-A-retz na-TAN liv-nay a-DAM

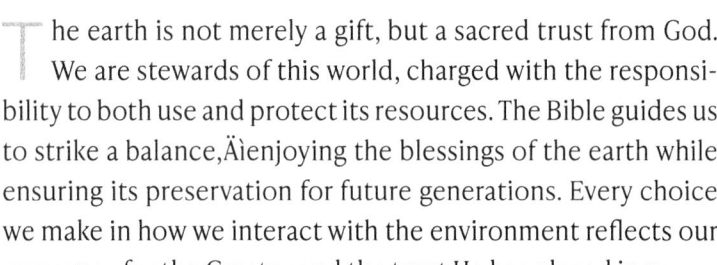

The earth is not merely a gift, but a sacred trust from God. We are stewards of this world, charged with the responsibility to both use and protect its resources. The Bible guides us to strike a balance‚Äìenjoying the blessings of the earth while ensuring its preservation for future generations. Every choice we make in how we interact with the environment reflects our reverence for the Creator and the trust He has placed in us.

R eflect on a time you made a conscious decision to protect or nurture the environment. How did this experience connect you to a deeper sense of responsibility and spirituality? In what ways can you further develop this balance in your daily life, ensuring that you honor the trust God has placed in you to care for the earth?

Seeing Through God's Eyes

"The stone that the builders rejected became a cornerstone."

PSALMS 118:22

E-ven ma-a-SU ha-bo-NEEM hai-TAH l'-ROSH pi-NAH

"The stone the builders rejected" is a reference to King David. Before he was anointed, David was overlooked and misunderstood, even by his own family. He wasn't seen as a candidate for leadership, yet he went on to become the cornerstone of Israel's royal house. We often overlook the strengths and potential of those around us, just as our own abilities might be ignored. But God sees what others may not, recognizing the unique potential within each of us.

Reflect on a time when you felt overlooked or underestimated. How did this experience shape your sense of self-worth? Consider how you might better recognize and appreciate the potential in yourself and others. How can you trust in God's awareness of your strengths, even when others may not see them?

Notes and Reflections

Notes and Reflections

Notes and Reflections